JAMESTOWN

Heritage

READERS

Book D

Lee Mountain, Ed.D.
University of Houston, Texas

Sharon Crawley, Ed.D.
Florida Atlantic University

Edward Fry, Ph.D.
Professor Emeritus
Rutgers University

Jamestown Publishers
Providence, Rhode Island

Favorite Children's Classics

ILLUSTRATED BY THE BEST ARTISTS
FROM THE PAST AND PRESENT

Jamestown Heritage Readers, Book D
Catalog No. 954
Catalog No. 954H, Hardcover Edition

Cover and text design by Deborah Hulsey Christie
Cover and border illustrations by Pamela R. Levy

Printed in the United States of America

3 4 5 6 HA 96 95 94 93

ISBN 0-89061-954-9
ISBN 0-89061-713-9, Hardcover Edition

C·O·N·T·E·N·T·S

ONE
Tales Retold

T W O
Here and There, Then and Now

UNIT ONE

Tales Retold

Bambi's Questions

from

BAMBI

by

FELIX SALTEN

n the early days of summer the trees stood still under the blue sky. Everything smelled of fresh leaves, of flowers, of wet grass and green wood.

These were the early days in the life of a deer named Bambi. He walked behind his mother on a path that ran through the bushes. How nice it was to walk there!

There were paths like that everywhere, running through the whole woods, and his mother knew them all. If Bambi sometimes stopped before a patch of bushes as if it were a green wall, she always found where the path went through.

Bambi questioned her. He loved to ask his mother questions. It was the nicest thing for him to ask a question and then to hear what answer his mother would give. Bambi was never surprised that question after question should come into his mind.

Sometimes, of course, he did not understand his mother's answer, but that was all right because he kept himself busy picturing what he had not understood, in his own way.

Once he asked, "Whom does this trail belong to, Mother?"

His mother answered, "To us."

Bambi asked again, "To you and me?"

"Yes," she said.

"To us two?" asked Bambi.

"Yes."

"Only to us two?" Bambi went on.

"No," said his mother. "To us deer."

"What are deer?" Bambi asked, and laughed.

His mother looked at him from head to foot and laughed too. "You are a deer, and I am a deer. We're both deer," she said. "Do you understand?"

Bambi leaped into the air for joy.
"Yes, I understand," he said. "I'm a little deer,
and you're a big deer, aren't you?"

His mother nodded and said, "Now you see."

But Bambi went on again. "Are there other deer
besides you and me?"

"Oh, yes," his mother said. "Lots of them."

"Where are they?" asked Bambi.

"Here, everywhere."

"But I don't see them," Bambi said.

"You will soon," his mother told him.

"When?" Bambi stood still, looking around.

"Soon." His mother walked on.

Bambi followed her. He was wondering what
"soon" might mean. He decided that "soon" was
certainly not "now." But he was not sure at what
time "soon" stopped being "soon" and began to be
"a long while."

13

Suddenly he asked, "Who made this trail?"

"We," his mother answered.

Bambi was surprised. "We? You and I?"

His mother said, "We . . . we deer."

Bambi asked, "Which deer?"

"All of us," his mother said.

As they walked on, Bambi was so happy that he felt like leaping off the path, but he stayed close to his mother.

Suddenly loud cries came from the top of a young tree that stood near their path. The mother deer went along without noticing, but Bambi stopped. Overhead two jays were screaming at each other.

"Get away," cried one. "I found this nest, and I found these eggs. They are mine to eat, so get away or I'll break your head for you."

"I'm not afraid of you," shouted the other jay.

The first jay spotted Bambi, and she flew down a few branches to scold at him. "What are you staring at?" she screamed.

Bambi leaped back, frightened. Quickly he caught up with his mother. He walked behind her again, thinking maybe she had not noticed that he had fallen behind.

After a bit, he started again. "Mother," he asked, "why were those jays so angry with each other?"

"They were fighting over food," she answered.

"Will we fight over food, too, sometime?" he asked.

"No," said his mother.

Bambi asked, "Why not?"

"Because there is enough for both of us," his mother replied.

15

Bambi wanted to know something else. "Mother," he began.

"What is it?"

"Will we get angry and scream at each other sometime?" he asked.

"No, child," said his mother. "We don't do such things."

They walked along again. Then something moved in front of them, close to the ground. The tall plants and grasses hid something that was running, springing. A sharp little cry rang out. Then all was still. A ferret had caught a mouse. He moved back through the grass, carrying it in his mouth.

"What was that?" asked Bambi.

"Nothing," said his mother.

"But," Bambi started. "But I saw it."

"Yes, yes," said his mother. "Don't be frightened. The ferret has killed a mouse."

But Bambi was frightened— frightened and worried and upset! It was quite a while before he could speak again.

Then he asked, "Why did the ferret kill the mouse?"

"Because." His mother did not go on. She acted as if she had answered the question.

Bambi thought about his next question. "Shall we kill a mouse, too, sometime?" he asked, worrying.

"No," replied his mother.

"Never?" asked Bambi.

"Never," came the answer.

"Why not?" asked Bambi, beginning to feel better.

"Because we never kill anything," said his mother.

❖ ❖ ❖ ❖

You can read more about Bambi and his friends in the book *Bambi* by Felix Salten.

17

My Breaking In

from

BLACK BEAUTY

by

ANNA SEWELL

I was still a colt, but my coat had grown fine and soft and was bright black. I had one white foot and a pretty white star on my head.

My master would not sell me until I was four years old. He said boys should not have to work like men, and colts should not have to work like horses until they were quite grown up.

When I was four years old, it was time for me to be broken in. My master said he would break me in himself, as he should not like me to be frightened or hurt.

19

Everyone may not know what breaking in is, so I will explain it. It means to teach a horse to wear a saddle and bridle and to carry on his back a man, woman, or child. The horse must learn to go just the way the rider wishes, and to go quietly.

Besides this, he has to learn to wear a collar, and he must stand still while it is put on. Then there is a cart fixed behind. He cannot walk or trot without dragging the cart after him. Also, he must go fast or slow, just as his driver wishes.

He must never start at what he sees, nor speak to other horses. Nor can he bite, nor kick, nor have any will of his own. He must always do his master's will, even though he may be very tired or hungry.

But the hardest of all is this. When his harness is once on, he may neither jump for joy nor lie down if he is tired. So you see this breaking in is a great thing.

I had, of course, long been used to wearing a halter so that I could be led about in the field. But now I was to have a bit and bridle. My master gave me some oats. After a good deal of patting and talking, he got the bit into my mouth and the bridle fixed. But it was a nasty thing!

Those who have never had a bit in their mouths cannot think how bad it feels.

It is a great piece of cold hard steel as thick as a man's finger. It is pushed into one's mouth, between one's teeth, and over one's tongue. The ends come out at the corners of your mouth. They are held fast there by straps over your head, under your throat, round your nose, and under your chin. In no way in the world can you get rid of the nasty hard thing. It is very bad! Yes, very bad!

But I knew my mother always had one on when she went out, and all horses did when they were grown up. So, what with the nice oats, and what with my master's pats, soft words, and kind ways, I got used to wearing my bit and bridle.

Next came the saddle, but that was not half so bad. My master put it on my back. Then he made the straps fast under my body, patting me and talking to me all the time. Then I had a few oats. Then a little leading about. And this he did every day until I began to look for the oats and the saddle when I saw him coming.

Finally, one morning, my master got on my back, and he rode me round the meadow on the soft grass. It certainly did feel strange. But I must say I felt rather proud to carry my master. Since he rode me a little every day, I soon became used to it.

The next part was putting on the iron shoes, and that too was very hard at first. My master went with me to the blacksmith. He wanted to be sure that I was not hurt or frightened.

The blacksmith took my feet in his hand, one after the other, and cut away some of the hoof. It did not hurt me, so I stood still on three legs until he had done them all.

Then he took a piece of iron the shape of my foot, and clapped it on. He drove some nails through the shoe quite into my hoof, so that the shoe was well on.

My feet felt very stiff and heavy, but in time I got used to it.

And now, having got so far, my master went on to break me to harness. There were more new things to wear. First, a stiff heavy collar on my neck, and then a bridle with great side pieces against my eyes called blinkers. And blinkers indeed they were, for I could not see on either side, but only straight in front of me.

Next there was a nasty stiff strap that went right under my tail. I hated that—to have my long tail pushed through that strap was almost as bad as the bit.

I never felt more like kicking. But of course I could not kick such a good master. So in time I got used to everything and could do my work as well as my mother.

I must not forget to tell about one other part of my training, which I have always thought was a great help to me. My master sent me for a while to stay with a neighboring farmer. The railway ran along one side of this farmer's meadow. In the meadow were some sheep and cows, and I was turned in among them.

I shall never forget the first train that ran by. I was feeding quietly near the fence, which stood between the meadow and the railway, when I heard a strange sound from far away.

Then it became louder and closer. Before I knew what was happening, there was a rush and a puffing out of smoke! A long black something flew by and was gone almost before I could draw my breath!

I turned and galloped to the far side of the meadow as fast as I could go, and there I stood, shaking with surprise and fear.

In the course of the day many other trains went by, some more slowly. One drew up close by and made a terrible noise before it stopped. But the cows went on eating quietly. They hardly raised their

heads as the loud black thing came puffing by.

For the first few days I could not even eat. But then I found that this terrible thing never came into the field, nor did it hurt me in any way. So I began to get used to it. Very soon I cared as little about the passing of a train as the cows and sheep did.

Since then I have seen many horses much frightened at the sight or sound of a train. But thanks to my good master's care, I am never upset or frightened at railways.

Now if anyone wants to break in a young horse well, that is the way.

After I was broken in, my master often drove me in harness with my mother. She was very well trained. So she could teach me how to go better than a strange horse could.

My mother told me the better I worked, the better

25

I should be cared for. She said it was wisest always to do my best to please my master.

"But," said she, "there are a great many kinds of men. There are good, kind men like our master. Any horse might be proud to work well for this kind of man. And there are bad men, who should never have a horse or dog to call their own.

"Besides, there are a great many men who are fools. They never trouble themselves to think. They spoil more horses than all, just for want of sense. They don't mean it, but they do it for all that.

"I hope you will fall into good hands, but a horse never knows who may buy it, or who may drive it. It is all a chance for us. But still I say, do your best whatever happens."

• • • •

You can read more about Black Beauty's adventures in the book *Black Beauty* by Anna Sewell.

The Milkmaid and Her Pail

from

AESOP'S FABLES

 young milkmaid was going to market, carrying her milk in a pail on her head. As she went along, she began thinking what she would do with the money she would get for the milk.

"I'll buy a chicken," said she, "and it will lay eggs for me. The eggs will hatch, and then I'll have more chickens. As soon as I have six chickens, I shall start selling eggs."

She smiled to herself, thinking about her plans. "With the money I get from selling eggs, I'll buy myself a new dress. Then, when I go to market, won't everyone come up and talk with me!"

Still thinking about the dress, she waved to some friends that she passed on the road. "I'll look so fine that all the girls from the city will be jealous, but I don't care. I shall just look at them and toss my head like this."

As she spoke, she tossed her head back. The pail fell off, and all the milk was spilled.

She went home, crying, and told her mother what had happened.

"There is no use crying over spilled milk," said her mother. "So dry your tears, my child."

Do not count your chickens before they are hatched.

Good Advice

by

LOUIS UNTERMEYER

Don't shirk
Your work
For the sake of a dream.
A fish
In the dish
Is worth two in the stream.

Ali Baba and the Forty Thieves

from the

ARABIAN NIGHTS

ong ago in a country called Persia there
lived a woodcutter named Ali Baba. He was not as
rich as his brother Kassim. But he worked hard and
lived happily with his wife, his son, and his servant
girl Morgiana.

One day Ali Baba went to cut wood in a part
of the forest he had never been to before. All
morning he worked alone in the quiet woods. Near
noon he heard the sound of galloping horses
coming toward him.

Fearing he may have happened onto someone
else's land, Ali Baba climbed a tree. He hid himself
high in the branches.

From his hiding place he could get a good look at
the band of riders who stopped in a clearing nearby.
They were a frightening sight to see, with daggers at
their belts.

31

"A good night's work," said one of them, waving his dagger in the air. "Two men met their end, and I am richer by two bags of gold."

"Would that I had done as well," said another. "For the killing of a whole family, I got only a few pieces of silver. So be it. Let us leave it off and get on our way."

Their captain walked over to a huge rock that stood near Ali Baba's hiding place. "Open, Sesame!" he cried in a loud voice, and a door opened in the rock.

One by one the robbers went in, carrying heavy sacks over their shoulders. Ali Baba counted them— forty men in all. The captain followed them inside, and the door closed behind him.

Fear kept Ali Baba still as a stone. He felt sure he would be killed if he were seen.

Soon the band of thieves came out again with their captain in the lead. Then all forty of them rode away.

It was still some time before Ali Baba felt brave enough to climb down from his hiding place, but once he was on the ground, he could not keep himself from taking a closer look at the rock. He ran his fingers over it but could feel no cracks. Yet he had seen a door open on the face of this very stone.

Then he remembered the words spoken by the captain of the thieves. In little more than a whisper, Ali Baba said, "Open, Sesame."

At once the secret door opened for him. Facing him was a sight that made him cry out in wonder. Huge piles of gold and silver! Boxes of fine clothes! Sacks of money! The sight of all these riches told him that the thieves must have been using this cave for years.

Ali Baba stepped inside for a closer look. Of itself, the door closed behind him.

His heart beat like that of a trapped animal.

Could he get out again? Would the words work from inside? He cried, "Open, Sesame."

The door opened again. Ali Baba picked up two sacks of gold, ran outside, and hurried home with them.

That night he emptied out the gold before his wife and told her all that had happened.

"What riches!" she exclaimed. "What joy! Let us count the gold, piece by piece."

"No, wife," said Ali Baba. "That will take too long. We must hurry to hide this gold. There is no time to be lost. I will dig a hole and bury the sacks."

"But we should make some count of how much gold is in each sack," she said. "I will go get the grain measure from the house of your brother Kassim. I will be back with it before you finish digging the hole."

"Say nothing of what you wish to measure," Ali Baba told his wife. "We want to keep this a secret."

"Not a word," she promised, and off she hurried to Kassim's house.

When she asked to use the grain measure, Kassim's wife was puzzled. Why would anyone want to measure grain so late at night?

She rubbed some sticky fat on the bottom of the measure before giving it to Ali Baba's wife. "Bring the measure back to me quickly," she said.

"I will," promised Ali Baba's wife. "Within the hour."

She was as good as her word. However, when she carried the measure back, she did not notice that a piece of gold had stuck to the fat on the bottom.

"Kassim," said his wife, as she showed him the piece of gold. "Your brother Ali Baba seems to be richer than we know. His wife does not count her gold. She measures it!"

"How can this be?" said Kassim. "I must talk with my brother."

When Kassim questioned him, Ali Baba knew he would have to share the secret. So he told his brother all, even the words for opening the door.

35

Early the next morning Kassim set out for the forest. He took with him ten mules bearing boxes and sacks that he meant to fill with gold.

When he reached the rock, he said, "Open, Sesame." The door opened at once and, when he was in, closed behind him.

Kassim hurried to fill sack after sack. "I will have more gold than the king," he said to himself.

His thoughts of riches pushed all other thoughts out of his mind. So, when it was time to open the door, Kassim was no longer thinking about the magic word.

"Open, Barley," he said.

The door stayed shut. What was wrong?

"Open, Barley," he shouted—and he waited.

Not even a tiny crack of light showed around the door.

It was a grain of some kind, thought Kassim. Not barley, but another grain. He had to remember.

"Open, Wheat," he tried.

Nothing happened.

Kassim's voice was shaking as he cried, "Open, Oats! Open!"

The name that mattered would not return to his mind. If he could not get the door to open, he would be caught inside.

"Open, Rye!" he screamed.

He was still inside, screaming and beating his head against the wall, when the thieves returned.

They saw Kassim's mules outside their cave. Their captain spoke the magic words, "Open, Sesame," and in they went.

They saw Kassim's sacks filled with their gold. They saw Kassim. And they quickly made an end of him before they left again.

When night came, and Kassim did not return from the forest, his wife grew more and more frightened. At last she went to Ali Baba and asked for his help.

37

So the next morning, Ali Baba set out on his mule to find his brother. And find him he did, right where the robbers had left his body.

Ali Baba stared in horror at the sight. But he knew he must get Kassim's body back to his home, and he must see that his brother was buried.

"We cannot let the truth be known about how my brother was killed," Ali Baba told Kassim's wife. "If we do, the robbers will track us down and kill our whole family. We must say only that he was taken sick and died."

So Ali Baba and his servant girl Morgiana washed and dressed the body, and they buried Kassim as quietly as they could.

Morgiana had lived in the house of Ali Baba since she was a child, so he knew she would keep his family's secret as if it were her own.

In the meantime, the robbers returned to their cave. Great was their surprise when they saw that the body of Kassim had been taken away.

"Someone has found us out," said their captain. "We must find him and kill him. But how to find him! One of us must go into the city and learn what family has just buried a man."

A young robber stepped forward. "I will go. I am a stranger to the city, and people feel they must answer the questions of a stranger. I will find the family we seek, and I will make a mark on their door."

In the city the robber quickly discovered that Ali Baba had just buried his brother. He made a mark on Ali Baba's door. Then he hurried back to the forest to tell the others.

"Well done," said the captain. "This afternoon we will go to the city in twos and threes. By dark we can make our way to the marked house, circle it, and kill everyone in it."

Earlier that same day, Ali Baba's servant girl Morgiana had left the house to buy some fruits. Upon her return, she saw the mark the robber had made on the door.

"This was not here when I left," she said. "And it

did not write itself. Someone has marked the house of Ali Baba, and it may be someone who means him no good. I will make this house harder to find."

So Morgiana went up and down the street. She marked every house in the same way that Ali Baba's house was marked.

As it grew dark, the thieves came together on Ali Baba's street, but they found themselves looking at one marked house after another.

"This will not do," shouted the captain. "Back to the forest, men. I will think of a better plan."

The next day the captain himself went into the city. He asked questions and found out where Kassim had been buried. Then he walked back and forth past Ali Baba's house until he was sure he could spot it again.

By the time the captain got back to his cave, he was ready to explain his plan. "Men," he said, "each of you must get a large oil jar with a wide neck. Such jars are big enough for a man to hide in. For Ali Baba, I am going to play the part of an oil merchant, taking these jars to market on my mules."

Some of the robbers nodded and started to smile. Others still looked puzzled.

"I will drive the mules past Ali Baba's house," the captain went on. "I will tell Ali Baba that I have traveled far and need to stay the night at his house. He cannot say no. But in the middle of the night, I will throw some stones at the oil jars. Then come out, with your daggers ready."

Soon the mules were on their way, carrying robbers in oil jars. The captain, dressed as an oil merchant, led them into the city, and he spoke to Ali Baba, as he had planned.

Ali Baba, believing the man was truly a stranger, opened his home to him. He told his servants to put the oil jars in his yard.

41

Soon the captain was having a fine dinner with Ali Baba.

In the kitchen the servant girl Morgiana needed some cooking oil, so she took a pot and went into the yard to get some. As she came near the first jar, she heard a voice inside say, "Is it time?"

Any other girl would have screamed. But not Morgiana! Bravely, she whispered, "Not yet," making her voice low, like a man's voice. Then she moved quickly from jar to jar. When she saw that there was a man hiding in each one, she knew what had to be done.

Morgiana put her biggest pot on the fire and filled it with water. She waited until it came to a fast boil. Then she went back and forth, pouring enough boiling water into each oil jar to make an end of the man hiding inside.

At midnight the captain got up as he had planned, and he threw some stones at the oil jars.

Nothing happened.

He ran to the yard and looked first into one jar, then another, then another. With growing horror, he saw that all his men had been killed. Fearing for his own life, he slipped out of Ali Baba's yard, and he ran along the dark streets until he was out of the city.

The next morning, the servant girl Morgiana told Ali Baba all that had happened—the mark on the door, the oil merchant, the men in the jars. And she explained all that she had done.

"You have saved my life," he cried. "You have saved the lives of all in this family. From this time forth, you are not our servant but our child."

Ali Baba buried the oil jars at the back of his yard. He hoped he had seen the last of the forty thieves, but that was not to be. The captain still had another plan.

He opened a shop near that of Ali Baba's son, and he took the name Hussain.

Ali Baba heard many good things about Hussain from his son, so one day he said, "Let us invite this good man to dinner."

When he came to the door, Morgiana looked at him closely. She felt she had seen his face before. Then she remembered. The oil merchant! Again she would have to save Ali Baba from the captain of the robbers. She made her plan.

Morgiana dressed herself in the clothes of a dancer. She put a band around her head to pull back her long hair. Then she hid a dagger under her skirt.

When the dinner was almost over, she asked leave of Ali Baba to dance for Hussain.

He nodded, clapped his hands, and called for music.

Morgiana sang as she circled the men, dancing faster and faster. The girl moved wildly into the dagger dance, swinging her skirt like the dancers of Persia. And suddenly, as she swung past Hussain, she buried her dagger deep in his heart.

"What have you done!" cried Ali Baba. "Morgiana, my child, what means this horror?"

"It means that you are safe from a man who came here to kill you," said Morgiana. "Hussain was no

friend to you or your son. Look well at his face, and
you will see the oil merchant. Look again, and you
will see the captain of the thieves."

She pulled back Hussain's shirt to show a hidden
dagger. "Look still again, and you will see what he
planned to drive into your heart."

"Once more you have saved me and mine!" said
Ali Baba, and he took Morgiana's hand and joined it
to the hand of his son. "Before, I named you my
child. Now, I hope to name you my daughter, the
wife of my son."

"Be it so," said the girl, and it was so.

Ali Baba kept away from the secret cave for a
whole year. Then, hoping it was no longer used by
robbers, he set forth to show the place to his son
and Morgiana.

As they came near it, Morgiana pointed out that
the ground near the cave was overgrown with grass
and plants. "No foot has stepped here," she said.
"We may enter safely."

Then the magic words "Open, Sesame" were
spoken. Those words were handed down to Ali
Baba's grandchildren and their grandchildren as
their passwords to riches.

45

Adventures of Isabel

from the poem by

OGDEN NASH

Isabel met an enormous bear.
Isabel, Isabel, didn't care.
The bear was hungry, the bear was ravenous,
The bear's big mouth was cruel and cavernous.
The bear said, Isabel, glad to meet you.
How do, Isabel, now I'll eat you!
Isabel, Isabel, didn't worry.
Isabel didn't scream or scurry.
She washed her hands and
she straightened
her hair up.
Then Isabel
quietly ate
the bear up.

Once in a night as black as pitch
Isabel met a wicked old witch.
The witch's face was cross and wrinkled.
The witch's gums with teeth were sprinkled.
Ho ho, Isabel! the old witch crowed,
I'll turn you into an ugly toad!
Isabel, Isabel, didn't worry.
Isabel didn't scream or scurry.
She showed no rage, she showed no rancor,
But she turned the witch into milk and drank her.

Isabel met a hideous giant.
Isabel continued self-reliant.
The giant was hairy, the giant was horrid,
He had one eye in the middle of his forehead.
Good morning, Isabel, the giant said,
I'll grind your bones to make my bread.
Isabel, Isabel, didn't worry.
Isabel didn't scream or scurry.
She nibbled the zwieback that she always fed off,
And when it was gone, she cut the giant's head off.

47

Bluebeard

by

CHARLES PERRAULT

here was once a man who was very rich. He had fine houses, both in town and in the country. He had much silver and gold, and he had clothes fit for a king. But this man also had a blue beard, which made him so ugly and terrible that all the women and girls ran away from him.

One of his neighbors, a fine lady, had two sons and two daughters. Both daughters were very beautiful. Bluebeard told his neighbor he would like to marry either one of the daughters. He said he would let her choose which one she would give to him.

But neither of them would have him. They sent him back and forth from one to the other, for neither girl wanted to marry a man who had a blue beard.

The blue beard was a problem, to be sure. But there was another problem, a strange and frightening problem, about Bluebeard. He had already married a number of wives, and nobody knew what had become of them.

Bluebeard took the girls, their mother, and some of their friends to his fine country home for a week. There was nothing going on but parties, hunting, fishing, and dancing. After such a week, the younger daughter began to think that this man's beard was not so very blue. So, when they returned home, she was married to Bluebeard.

About a month later Bluebeard told his wife that he had to leave on a trip. "Invite your family to stay

49

with you, and have your friends come too," he said. "I want you to live well while I am gone."

Then he took his big heavy key ring out of his pocket. "Here are all my keys," he said. "This key is for the room where I keep my silver and gold. This one opens my safe, which holds my money. This thin key is for my house in the city, and these larger ones are for the rooms in this house. But as for this little key, it is the key to the closet at the end of the hall on the ground floor."

His wife took the key ring with a smile.

"Open all the doors," Bluebeard went on. "Go everywhere. But as for that closet, do not enter it. Do not use that little key. I promise you surely that if you open that closet door, you will have much to fear from me."

She promised to do exactly as he said, so he left on his trip.

Her sister came to stay with her, and her brothers stopped by for visits. She shared the riches of her house with many of her friends, but all these riches did not make this young wife happy.

More and more she thought about the little key. Why had Bluebeard told her not to use it? She would

often slip away and walk up and down the hall that led to the closet door, wondering why she should not go in there.

Finally she could stand it no longer. She took the little key and opened the door of the closet.

At first she could not make out anything plainly because it was so dark, but after a minute she could see that the closet was as large as a room. And on the floor of the closet were the heads and bodies of a number of dead women.

These were the other women Bluebeard had married. She knew now that he had killed them, one after the other, and he had hidden them in this closet.

She thought she should surely die for fear, and the key, which she pulled out of the lock, fell out of her hand. When she stopped shaking, she picked up the key and locked the door. Then she went upstairs, but she could not rest because she was so frightened.

Seeing that the key of the closet was stained, she tried to rub off the stain, but it would not come out. She washed the key. She even took that key off the ring and rubbed it with sand, but the stain was still there, for the key was a magic key. She could never make it quite clean. When the stain was gone from one side, it came again on the other.

Bluebeard returned from his trip that same day. He asked for his keys. His wife gave them to him, but her hand was shaking, and she looked at him with great fear in her eyes. At once he knew what had happened.

"How is it," said he, "that the key of my closet is not with the rest?"

"I must certainly have left it upstairs on the table," said she.

"Bring it to me," said Bluebeard.

So she had to bring him the key.

Bluebeard looked at it. Then he said to his wife, "What made this stain upon the key?"

"I do not know," cried the poor woman.

"You do not know!" said Bluebeard. "I very well know. You wished to go into the closet? Very well, you shall go in, and you shall take your place with the ladies you saw there."

She threw herself at Bluebeard's feet and begged for her life.

But he only shook his head.

"You must die," he said. "At once."

She looked at him with tears in her eyes. "Since I must die," said she, "give me a little time to say my prayers."

"I will give you half an hour," said he. "But not one minute more!"

When she was alone, she called out to her sister whose name was Anne. "Go up, I beg you, to the top of the tower, sister Anne. See if our brothers are coming. They promised me they would come today. If you see them, give them a sign to hurry."

Her sister Anne went up to the top of the tower.

The poor wife cried out from time to time, "Anne! Sister Anne, do you see anyone coming?"

Sister Anne said, "I see nothing but the sun, which makes a dust, and the grass, which looks green."

Meanwhile Bluebeard, holding a great sword in his hand, cried out to his wife, "Come down now, or I shall come up and get you."

"One minute longer, if you please," said his wife. Then she cried out very softly, "Anne, sister Anne! Do you see anyone coming now?"

Again sister Anne answered, "I still see nothing but the sun, which makes a dust, and the grass, which is green."

"Come down quickly," cried Bluebeard. "Or I will come up to you."

"I am coming," answered his wife. Then she cried, "Anne, sister Anne. Look again. Do you see anyone coming?"

"I see," said sister Anne, "a great dust, which comes from this side."

"Are they our brothers?"

"Alas, no, my sister. They are sheep."

"Will you not come down?" cried Bluebeard.

"One minute longer," said his wife. Then she cried out, "Anne, sister Anne. Look once more, I beg you. Do you see anyone coming?"

"I see two horsemen," said she. "But they are a great way off."

"They are our brothers," said the poor wife with a cry of joy. "Make them a sign, as well as you can, for them to ride faster."

Then Bluebeard shouted so loudly that he made the whole house shake.

His wife came down and threw herself at his feet. She was all in tears, with her hair about her shoulders.

"All this is of no help to you," said Bluebeard. "You must die." Then taking hold of her with one hand, and lifting his sword into the air with the other, he was ready to take off her head.

The poor lady turned about to him, and looking at him with tears in her eyes, she asked him to give her one little minute more for her prayers.

"No, no!" he said, and again lifting his arm—

At that second there was such a loud knocking at the gate that Bluebeard stopped suddenly. The gate was opened, and in ran two horsemen. With swords in their hands, they rushed at Bluebeard. He knew them to be his wife's brothers.

He ran away, but the two brothers overtook him before he could get out of the house. They ran their swords through his body and left him dead. The poor wife was almost as dead as Bluebeard. She had not strength enough to get up and welcome her brothers.

Bluebeard had no children, so all his riches went to his wife. She gave some to her sister Anne and some to her brothers. She shared the rest with a fine and kind man whom she married, and he helped her to forget the sorry time she had passed with Bluebeard.

I Am Colin

from

THE SECRET GARDEN

by

FRANCES HODGSON BURNETT

 ary Lennox was awakened in the night by
the sound of rain beating with heavy drops against
her window. It was pouring. The wind was moaning
round the corners and in the chimneys of the huge
old house. Mary felt miserable and angry as she
listened to the wind.

"It sounds just like a person who is lost,
wandering on and on, crying," she thought.

She lay awake, turning from side to side, for about
an hour. Suddenly something made her sit up in bed
and turn her head toward the door, listening. Mary
Lennox listened and she listened.

59

"It isn't the wind now," she whispered to herself. "I'm sure that is not the wind. It's different. It's that crying I've heard before in this house."

The door of her room was open a crack, and the sound came from down the hall, a far-off sound of crying. Mary listened for a few minutes, and each minute she became more and more certain. She felt as if she must find out what it was. It seemed even stranger than the secret garden and the buried key.

This strange house was full of secrets. She put her feet out of bed and stood on the floor.

"I am going to find out what it is," she said to

herself as she put on her woolly robe. Mary picked
up the candle by her bedside and went softly out of
the room.

The hall looked very long and dark, but she
was too excited to mind that. She thought she
remembered the corners she must turn to find the
short hall with the door covered with tapestry—the
one she had seen open and close the day she lost
herself in this huge old house.

The sound had come up that hall, so Mary went
on with her candle, almost feeling her way. Her
hand was shaking, so the candle threw strange
shadows on the walls.

The far-off crying went on and led her. Sometimes
it stopped for a minute or so. Then it began again.
Was this the right corner to turn? Mary stopped and
thought. Yes, it was. Down this hall and then to the
left, then up two steps and to the right again. Yes,
there was the tapestry door.

She pushed it open very softly and closed it
behind her. She stood in the hall and could hear
the crying plainly now, though it was not loud.
It was on the other side of the wall at her left. A few
yards farther on, there was a door, and she could see

61

a line of light below the door. The Someone was crying in that room.

Mary walked to the door. She pushed it open, and there she was, standing in that room!

It was a big room with a low fire in the fireplace. There was a candle burning on a fine old table beside a big four-posted bed, and on the bed was lying a boy, crying.

Mary wondered if she was in a real place or if she had fallen asleep again and was dreaming without knowing it.

The boy had a thin face. He seemed to have eyes too big for it. His heavy locks of hair made his face seem smaller. He looked like he had been very sick, but he was crying more as if he were tired and cross than as if he were sick.

Mary stood near the door with her candle in her hand, holding her breath. Then she walked softly across the room.

As she drew nearer, the boy turned his head. He stared at her, his gray eyes opening so wide that they seemed huge.

"Who are you?" he said at last, in a half-frightened whisper. "Are you a ghost?"

"No, I am not," Mary answered, her own whisper sounding half frightened. "Are you one?"

He stared and stared and stared.

"No," he answered after waiting a few seconds. "I am Colin."

"Who—who is Colin?" she stammered.

"I am Colin Craven. Who are you?"

"I am Mary Lennox. Mr. Craven is my uncle."

"He is my father," said the boy.

"Your father!" cried Mary. "No one ever told me he had a boy! Why didn't they?"

"Come here," he said, still keeping his strange eyes fixed on her.

She came close to the bed, and he put out his hand and touched her.

"You are real, aren't you?" he said. "I have such dreams very often. You might be one of them."

Mary had put on a woolly robe before she left her room. She put a piece of the cloth between his fingers.

"Rub that and see how warm it is," she said. "I will pinch you a little if you like, to show you how real I am. For a minute I thought you might be a dream too."

"Where did you come from?" he asked.

"From my own room," said Mary. "I couldn't sleep, and I heard someone crying and wanted to find out who it was. What were you crying for?"

"Because I couldn't sleep either," said Colin, "and my head hurt. Tell me your name again."

"Mary Lennox. Did no one ever tell you I had come to live here?"

"No," he answered. "They would not."

"Why?" asked Mary.

"Because I should have been afraid you would see me. I won't let people see and talk about me."

"Why?" Mary asked again, feeling more puzzled every minute.

"Because I am like this always, sick, and having to lie down. If I live to grow up, I may be a hunchback. My father won't let people talk about me either. No one who works here is allowed to speak of me, not the cook, not the gardener, not even the nurse."

"Oh, what a strange house this is!" Mary said. "Everything is a secret. Rooms are locked up, and gardens are locked up—and you! Have you been locked up?"

65

"No," said Colin. "I stay in this room because I don't want to be moved out of it. It tires me too much."

"Does your father come and see you?" Mary asked.

"Sometimes, but mostly when I am asleep. He doesn't want to see me."

"Why?" Mary could not help asking again.

An angry shadow passed over the boy's face. "My mother died when I was born, and it makes him miserable to look at me. He thinks I don't know, but I've heard people talking. He almost hates me."

"He hates the garden because she died," said Mary, half speaking to herself.

"What garden?" the boy asked.

"Oh, just—just a garden she used to like," Mary stammered. "Have you been here always?"

"Nearly always. Sometimes I have been taken to places at the sea, but I won't stay because people stare at me. I used to wear an iron thing to keep my back straight, but a doctor from the city came to see me and said it was doing no good. He told them to take it off and keep me out in the fresh air, but mostly I stay inside here because I don't like people to see me."

Mary thought of something, all at once. "If you don't like people to see you," she began, "do you want me to go away?"

He still held the fold of her robe, and he gave it a little pull.

"No," he said. "I should be sure you were a dream if you went away. If you are real, sit down on that chair and talk. I want to hear about you."

Mary put down her candle on the table near the bed and sat down. She did not want to go away at all. She wanted to stay in the hidden-away room and talk to the strange boy.

"What do you want me to tell you?" she said.

He wanted to know how long she had been at his father's house. He wanted to know which hall her room was on. He wanted to know where she had lived before. She answered all these questions

67

and many more as he lay back and listened. He made her tell him all about living in India and about her trip back to England.

She found out that because he had been sick, he had not learned things as other children had. One of his nurses had taught him to read when he was quite little, so he was always reading books. Though his father did not visit much, he was given anything he asked for, and he was never made to do anything he did not like to do.

"Everyone has been told to do what pleases me," he said. "It makes me sick to be angry. No one believes I shall live to grow up."

He said it as if he was so used to the idea that it no longer mattered to him at all. He seemed more interested in asking Mary questions than in talking about whether he would live.

"How old are you?" he said.

"I am ten," answered Mary. "And so are you."

"How do you know that?" he asked in a surprised voice.

"Because when you were born, the garden door was locked, and the key was buried. It has been locked up for ten years."

Colin half sat up, turning toward her.

"What garden door was locked? Who did it? Where was the key buried?" he exclaimed as if he were suddenly very much interested.

"It—it was the garden Mr. Craven hates," Mary said in little more than a whisper. "He locked the door. No one—no one knows where he buried the key."

"What sort of garden is it?" Colin asked.

"No one has been allowed to go into it for ten years," was Mary's careful answer.

But it was too late to be careful. He was too much like herself. He too had had nothing to think about, and the idea of a hidden garden excited him as it had excited her. He asked question after question.

Where was it? Had she ever looked for the door? Had she asked the gardeners?

"They won't talk about it," said Mary. "I think they have been told not to answer questions."

"I would make them," said Colin. "Everyone has to please me. I told you that. If I were to live, this place would sometime belong to me. They all know that. I would make them tell me."

Mary had not known that she herself had been spoiled, but she could see quite plainly that this strange boy had been. He thought he had a right to make everyone do as he wished. How strange he was, and how coolly he spoke of not living.

"Do you think you won't live?" Mary asked.

"I don't suppose I shall," he said, as if he didn't really care.

"Do you want to live?"

"No," Colin answered in a cross, tired way, "but I don't want to die either. When I feel sick, I lie here and think about it, and then I cry."

"I have heard you crying three times," Mary said, "but I did not know who it was. Were you crying about that?"

"I guess so," he answered. "Let us talk about

something else. Talk about that hidden garden. Don't you want to see it?"

"Yes," answered Mary, in quite a low voice.

"I do," he went on. "I don't think I ever really wanted to see anything before, but I want to see that garden. I want the key dug up, and I want the door opened. I would make them take me there. That would be getting fresh air. I am going to make them open the door, and I will let you come along."

Colin had become quite excited, and his eyes began to shine like stars. They looked bigger than ever.

"Oh, don't—don't—don't do that," she cried, afraid that everything about the garden would be spoiled, and she would never again feel like a bird with a safe-hidden nest.

He stared at her as if he thought she were not making sense.

"Why?" he said. "You said you wanted to see it."

"I do," she said. "But if you make them open the door and take you in like that, it will never be a real secret again."

He leaned still farther forward. "A real secret," he said. "What do you mean? Tell me."

71

"You see, if no one knows but the two of us—if there was a door, hidden somewhere, and we could find it—just think. We could slip through it and shut it behind us. No one would know there was anyone there, and we could call it our garden, and if we played there, and dug and planted seeds, we could make things grow. Don't you see? Oh, don't you see how much nicer it would be if it was a secret?"

Colin sat up with a strange look on his face. "I never had a secret," he said, "except that one about not living to grow up. They don't know I know that, so it's kind of a secret, but I like this kind better."

Mary began to feel better because the idea of keeping the secret seemed to please him. She felt almost sure she could make him see the garden in his mind as she had seen it. Then, like her, he would not be able to bear thinking that just anyone could go into the garden anytime. It should be theirs.

"I'll tell you what I *think* the garden would be like, if we could go into it," she said. "It has been shut up so long that things would have grown wild. All weeds and flowers and tall grasses coming up together! Vines *might* have climbed from tree to tree and hung down. Birds *might* have built their nests

there in low bushes because it was so safe."

"I didn't know birds might do that," he said. "But if you stay in a room, you never see things. What a lot of things you know! I feel as if you had been inside that garden."

Mary did not know what to say, so she did not say anything, but he did not seem to be waiting for an answer. He seemed to be thinking and planning.

At last he said, "You must look each day for the garden door. When you come here, you can tell me about where you have looked. It will be our secret."

He lay thinking again, as he had done before. "I think *you* shall be a secret, too, for now. I will not tell them yet. I can always send my nurse out and say

73

that I want to be by myself. Come back tomorrow night. By then I'll think of a way to let you know when I am alone."

His eyes looked excited still, but heavy.

"I've been here a long time," said Mary. "Shall I go away now? You look tired."

"I wish I could go to sleep before you leave me," he said.

"Shut your eyes," said Mary, drawing her chair closer to the bed. "I will do what the nurses used to do in India. I will pat your hand and sing something quite low." So she sang a soft little song.

"That is nice," he said, and she went on singing in a whisper. When she looked at him again, he was fast asleep.

Mary got up softly, took her candle, and slipped away without making a sound.

Hope

by

LANGSTON HUGHES

Sometimes when I'm lonely,
Don't know why,
Keep thinkin' I won't be lonely
By and by.

The Falcon and the Chicken

by

LEO TOLSTOY

here was once a falcon who was a fine hunting bird. This falcon worked well for his master. He would hop up and sit on the back of his master's hand when he was called.

A chicken was kept by the same master, but the chicken would run away whenever the master reached out to him.

"It isn't right," the falcon said to the chicken. "You always run from our master, except at feeding time. I go to him of my own free will when I am called. I don't forget that he feeds me, and I am grateful. Why are you not grateful? Why do you run away from our master? I never run from him."

The chicken cocked her head to one side. "You never run because you have never seen baked falcon on the master's dinner table. From time to time, I have seen baked chicken."

Chanticleer and the Fox

from

THE CANTERBURY TALES

by

GEOFFREY CHAUCER

nce there was a woman who had two daughters, three pigs, a sheep, *and* one prize rooster. The rooster's name was Chanticleer. Chanticleer was a fine-looking rooster. His comb was bright red. His bill was black and shiny, and his feathers were the colors of the rainbow.

No other rooster was better than Chanticleer when it came to crowing. His "cock-a-doodle-doo" was louder than the church bells and always on time. Each morning he woke the people for miles around.

Chanticleer felt a great love for one special hen. Her name was Pertelote. She had won Chanticleer's heart when they were both just chicks.

Now it happened that one morning before the first light Chanticleer cried out in his sleep. Pertelote, close beside him, woke with a start.

She shook Chanticleer. "Wake up, my dear! You must have been dreaming a terrible dream."

"Indeed I was, my lady," said Chanticleer. "My heart is still racing. I dreamed I met an animal who looked much like a dog, and he wanted to grab me and kill me. His color was golden brown with black markings on his ears and tail. Oh, the very thought of him still makes me shake with fear."

Pertelote laughed. "I don't know what to think of you—to be so frightened by a dream! There is nothing to be afraid of in dreams!"

"There are many stories of dreams that had a meaning," said Chanticleer.

Pertelote shook her head. "The bad dream you had tonight must have been brought on by something you ate. Maybe you need some nice fresh worms this morning to settle your stomach."

"You may be right," said Chanticleer. "Still, I have a strong feeling that this dream of mine means some trouble is coming to me. But enough of that! Let's turn to happier thoughts."

Chanticleer stood up and flapped his wings. "Dear Pertelote, when I look at your lovely face— you do have such beautiful red circles around your eyes—it makes me forget my bad dream."

With those words he flew down to the ground.

Now it was day. And he was not afraid of anything. He threw back his head and crowed "Cock-a-doodle-doo" at the top of his voice.

But a terrible thing was about to happen to him.

That night, while he had been dreaming, a fox had broken into the farmyard. He was hiding in the bushes near where Chanticleer and the hens would feed. There he lay, still and quiet, waiting.

While Pertelote and the other hens were flapping around, Chanticleer walked ahead, singing happily. He happened to look over at a butterfly about to light on a leaf. And just as he did, he spotted the fox.

Chanticleer gave a start and broke off his song. He knew that he was looking at the animal of his dream!

Chanticleer wanted to run away.

But before he could move, the fox said, "I am a friend. Surely you aren't afraid of me? I would never hurt you. It is widely known that you have a fine voice. I came here only to hear you sing."

These words made Chanticleer feel better. He knew his voice was fine. Maybe there was no reason for him to be afraid.

"I have heard that your best notes come forth when you close your eyes and stand on your toes," the fox went on. "Do stand tall, and stretch out your neck for me. Let me hear you sing in a voice that is loud and strong."

Proudly, Chanticleer raised himself up. He closed his eyes, stretched out his neck, and began to crow.

But on his first note, the fox leaped. Grabbing Chanticleer by the neck, the fox ran for the woods.

Just then, Pertelote saw what was happening. She set up a cry loud enough to be heard in the farm house.

The noise brought the woman and her two daughters. They rushed over just in time to see the fox running across the field, carrying Chanticleer away.

"Help!" cried the woman. Taking up a stick, she ran after the fox.

The people in the next field heard her and came running. Behind them came their dogs, and then the pigs, and even the sheep.

The dogs barked. The men and women shouted.

Hearing all this noise, Chanticleer took courage. "Sir Fox," he said, as best he could with his neck in the fox's mouth. "Why don't you tell those silly people to go back home? They can't catch you. Now that you are near the woods, you could say to them, 'I have your rooster, and I am going to eat him.' "

"That is right," thought the fox, and he opened his mouth to speak.

But that very second, Chanticleer flapped his wings and flew right up to the top of a tree.

The fox, too late, saw that Chanticleer was free. "Dear friend," he said softly. "I must have frightened you when I took you up so suddenly. Truly I was carrying you away from your farmyard only because I wanted you to visit my home. Do come down, and let me show you where I live. I hoped you would sing for me there, since I so love your fine voice."

"Come down?" said Chanticleer. "Not I! Your sweet words cannot trick me a second time. Never again will I be so fooled. There is no hope for one who closes his eyes just when he needs most to see."

"Well," sighed the fox. "There is just as little hope for one who talks when he should keep his mouth shut, so each of us has learned a lesson. Good day!"

Be Like the Bird

by

VICTOR HUGO

Be like the bird, who
Halting in his flight
On limb too slight
Feels it give way beneath him,
Yet sings,
Knowing he hath wings.

The Life of a Man Is a Circle

by

BLACK ELK, LAKOTA SIOUX

The life of a man is a circle from childhood to childhood, and so it is in everything where power moves. Our teepees were round like the nests of the birds, and these were always set in a circle, the nation's hoop, a nest of many nests, where the Great Spirit meant for us to hatch our children.

86

Dust of Snow

by

ROBERT FROST

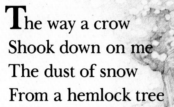

The way a crow
Shook down on me
The dust of snow
From a hemlock tree

Has given my heart
A change of mood,
And saved some part
Of a day I had rued.

87

UNIT TWO

Here and There,
Then and Now

The Pale Pink Dog

from

HENRY HUGGINS

by

BEVERLY CLEARY

Henry learns that there will be a dog show in the park on Saturday. He decides to enter his dog, Ribsy, in the show. Ribsy is a mongrel, which is a dog of mixed breeds. But that doesn't stop Henry from thinking that Ribsy can win the silver cup.

Henry meets his friends and tells them the news. They decide to enter their dogs too.

The day of the dog show finally arrives. Henry gives Ribsy a bath and uses a piece of clothesline for a leash.

The story begins as Henry leaves his house with Ribsy and meets his friends on the way to the dog show.

hen Henry went out on the front porch, he saw Beezus and Ramona coming down the street. Beezus was carrying a squirming black puppy that kept trying to lick her face. "Puddles, you stop that!" she commanded and set him on the sidewalk. Puddles was wearing a red bow on his collar and Henry was pleased to see that Ribsy wasn't the only dog with a rope for a leash.

"Come on, Henry, we'd better hurry," said Beezus.

Ribsy sniffed at the puppy and decided to ignore him. "Hey, look," exclaimed Henry. "There's Mary Jane and Patsy and Robert and Sassy up there ahead. We'd better run."

When they reached the park, Henry saw that already there were hundreds of boys and girls and dogs there ahead of them. Henry had never seen so many dogs. There were boxers, Great Danes, Pekingese, Airedales, cockers, Saint Bernards, Pomeranians, beagles, setters, pointers, and just plain dogs. Some, like Puddles, were wearing ribbons on their collars, some wore sweaters, and some had on little paper hats.

A loud-speaker on a sound truck blared out. "Take your entry blanks to the registration desk by the tennis courts."

"Come on, Ribsy." Henry found his way through the crowds of children and dogs to the registration desk. There he waited in line to weigh Ribsy on a big scale. At first Ribsy didn't want to be weighed, but Henry and a boy scout managed to shove him upon the scale and keep him still long enough to see that he weighed twenty-eight pounds.

"You've grown a lot heavier in a year," said Henry. "Maybe we shouldn't call you Ribsy any more."

After the dog was weighed, a lady gave Henry a yellow cardboard arm band. It had "Woofies Dog Food—Woofies make dogs woof for joy" printed on it. Below that there was a space for the kind of dog, weight-class, and the ring in which the dog was to be shown. The lady wrote on it, "Mixed breed—25 to 40 pounds—Ring 3."

Henry led Ribsy toward a sign with "Ring 3" printed on it over by a flower bed. Ribsy stopped to shake himself and then, before Henry knew what was happening, he dashed over to the flower bed and rolled in the dirt.

"Hey, cut that out!" yelled Henry. "You're getting all dirty."

It was too late. Henry pulled Ribsy, streaked with mud, out of the flowers. Henry tried to brush off the dirt. Then he tried to rub it off with his handkerchief. He only smeared it. He was discouraged. Why had he bragged so much about his dog? Now he would never win a prize.

When Henry reached Ring 3, he saw that it was made of rope tied to four stakes driven into the ground. Inside was a table piled with the prizes Henry had read about. Henry looked at the silver cup and thought it would look nice on his dresser. Not that he had a chance with a muddy dog. He noticed some of the boys had brought brushes and were brushing their dogs. He wished he had thought to bring a brush.

The day was warm. Henry sat down on the grass with the rest of the boys and girls to wait for the judging to start. He kept trying to brush some of the dirt off Ribsy. In the ring next to his he saw a snow-white dog. Somebody said it was a Siberian sled dog. The dog's owner was brushing him and sprinkling white powder on him to make him look whiter.

Henry had an idea! If he only had time, he could run home for a can of talcum powder to sprinkle on the white parts of Ribsy! That would cover up the dirt. It didn't matter about the yellow and black and brown parts. The dirt didn't show there much.

Just then the voice boomed over the loud-speaker. "We are going to postpone the judging for a little while, because we have a real treat for all you kids. Maud, the trained mule, is going to entertain you."

The children all started toward the truck to see Maud. That is, all except Henry. He was not interested in any trained mule. He wanted Ribsy to win a silver cup. Here was his chance. He could run home and back while Maud the mule performed.

"Come on, Ribsy!" he yelled. "We have to step on it."

Followed by Ribsy, he ran as fast as he could out of the park and up the hill to his house on Klickitat Street. He rushed into his room and snatched his hairbrush. He tore into the bathroom and grabbed a can of talcum powder. Then he rushed back to the park with Ribsy. The children were still crowded around Maud.

Henry was so hot and sticky that he had to sit down on the grass to catch his breath. Ribsy was panting and his tongue hung out. Henry brushed him with the hairbrush. That helped a little. Then he sprinkled powder on the big white spot on his back.

Henry was horrified. He could scarcely believe what he saw. The talcum powder wasn't white—it was pink! Who ever heard of a dog with pink spots! Quickly he tried to brush the powder off. But Ribsy was still damp and the powder didn't brush off.

Henry decided to make all Ribsy's white parts pink so they would match. Maybe in the bright sunshine the judges wouldn't notice. He sprinkled powder on Ribsy's white ear and left hind paw. He even sprinkled some on his white tail. Yes, Ribsy did look better with all his light parts matching. Maybe the judges would wear dark glasses.

Maud finished her act and the children came back to the rings with their dogs. "Hey, look at the pink dog!" a boy exclaimed.

"I never heard of a pink dog," a girl said. "What kind is he?"

"He's a mixed breed," said Henry.

He put the talcum powder can in his pocket and decided not to say anything about it. Maybe the others would think he had some rare breed of dog.

A man stood in the center of the ring. Henry noticed that he was not wearing dark glasses. "All right," the man called. "Bring your dogs into the ring and march them around in single file."

"Come on, Ribsy, they're going to start judging. You'd better behave yourself." Henry led him by the clothesline into the ring.

The children walked their dogs around in a circle. Ribsy's long rope tangled with the other dogs' leashes. Finally the judge directed them to stop. "Now get your dogs ready," he ordered.

Henry didn't know what he meant, so he watched the others. Some of them knelt by their dogs and made them stand still and look ahead.

That must be what the judge meant. Henry knelt beside Ribsy. Ribsy sat down. He opened his mouth and let his long pink tongue hang out. He was thirsty.

"Come on, Ribs, stand up," begged Henry. "Be a good dog." Ribsy began to pant. "Come on, get up!"

Ribsy lay down on the grass and panted harder. Henry pulled and tugged. He looked over his shoulder at the judge. The judge was looking at the ears and teeth of a dog that was standing properly. Then he ran his hands over the dog. The dog didn't move.

"Come on, Ribsy!" begged Henry. "It'll be our turn pretty soon." Ribsy closed his eyes. "I know you're thirsty. I'll get you a drink of water just as soon as I can."

The loud-speaker made an announcement.

97

"Will the boy scouts please take pans of water to each ring?"

Henry was relieved to see a boy scout coming with water, but when Ribsy's turn came, he sniffed at the pan and refused to drink.

"I guess he's used to his own dishes," explained Henry. "He just doesn't want to use the same pan as the other dogs."

"Can't help it," said the boy scout. "It's the only one I have."

Ribsy continued to pant.

At last the judge came to Henry. "Well, well, a pink dog," he exclaimed.

"Yes, sir," said Henry.

"Come on, son. Stand him up."

Henry boosted Ribsy to his feet. Ribsy tried to sit down again, but Henry held up his hind end by the tail. The judge looked at his ears and teeth. Then he ran his hands over him. He looked at his fingers afterward. They were pink. "Hmmmm," he said.

When the judge had looked at all the dogs, he ordered each child to walk across the ring and back with his dog.

Henry noticed that the boys and girls who knew about these things held the leash in the left hand. When his turn came he held the clothesline in his left hand and started across the ring.

Halfway across, Ribsy sat down to scratch behind his left ear. Henry pulled at the rope. When he reached the other side of the ring and turned back, Ribsy turned the wrong way so that he crossed in front of Henry.

Henry tripped on the rope and started to change it to his right hand, but just then Ribsy ran around behind Henry to growl at a dog that was mostly spaniel.

The boy who owned the spaniel pulled him away and started to the other side of the ring. Ribsy ran in front of Henry and pulled at his rope to get closer to the other dog. The harder he pulled, the tighter the rope drew around Henry's legs.

The children began to laugh. Ribsy was so excited he ran around behind Henry and pulled the rope even tighter. The laughter increased.

"Cut that out, Ribsy!" Henry ordered, looking over his shoulder at his dog. He felt silly standing there wound up in a clothesline.

"Come on, son," said the judge. "We can't waste time. A lot of other boys and girls want to show their dogs, too."

Now, on top of all his troubles, the judge was cross with him. Henry knew a cross judge would never give him a silver cup. Discouraged and feeling even sillier, Henry twirled around like a top to unwind himself from the rope. Relieved to have that part of the show over, he dragged Ribsy to the side of the ring. In a few minutes he could take his dog home and give him a drink.

After each child had walked his dog, the judge went around the ring pointing to different boys and girls, saying, "All right, you stay in the ring." He looked at Henry and his dog. "Hmmmm," he said. "All right, you stay in."

As the contestants left the ring, the boy scouts handed them prizes. Those who left first won the smallest prizes. The longer they stayed in the ring, the bigger the prize.

"Hey, Henry, are you still in?" Henry looked up. Robert and Sassy were standing outside the rope.

"Yes," answered Henry, "and I sure don't see why. Ribsy did everything wrong. Did Sassy win anything?"

"Just a dog whistle." Robert took another look at Ribsy. "Say, how did he get all pink?"

"Aw, mind your own beeswax," said Henry. He pretended to be watching the judge carefully. One by one the man asked the boys and girls to leave the ring.

"Look what I won!" Henry saw Beezus waving a rubber mouse. "See, it squeaks!" She squeaked it. Then she stopped. "Look!" she squealed. "Ribsy is pink!"

"Shut up!" Henry looked at the judge. He wished he knew why he was staying in the ring. Every time the judge passed him he looked at Ribsy and said, "Hmmmm. Stay in the ring."

Mary Jane was the next one to see him. "See, I won a pillow for Patsy to sleep on," she said and then looked at Ribsy. "Why, Henry Huggins! What did you do to that poor dog? He's all pink. Just wait till your mother finds out about this."

"You keep quiet!" Henry said fiercely. There were only a few left in the ring.

Scooter was last to arrive. "Hi, Henry," he said. "Are you and that old mutt still in the ring? The judge must be blind. I guess Rags is a pretty good dog. Just the best in his class is all, and now he has to go to another ring to compete for the best dog in the show." He held up a small silver cup. Like the others, he looked at Ribsy. "I must be seeing things! A pink dog!" Scooter began to laugh. He sat down on the grass, laughing so hard he rolled back and forth.

Henry didn't think Ribsy was that funny. By this time Henry was so hot and disgusted that all he wanted was to get out of the ring, go home, and get Ribsy a drink of water out of his own private pan.

"Hmmmm," said the judge again.

At last only Henry and another boy were left. Henry remembered that the other boy's dog had done all the right things.

The judge stepped to the center of the ring with a silver cup in his hand. Henry wasn't at all surprised when the judge handed it to the other boy. He just wondered why he hadn't been asked to leave the ring. He thought he must have made a mistake, but the judge said to Henry and the winner, "Come along to the main ring. There will be some more judging there."

Puzzled, Henry followed. Beezus and Ramona,
Scooter, Mary Jane, and Robert, and their dogs
followed Henry. Maybe Henry was going to win a
prize after all.

In the main ring were the prize winners from all the
other rings. Henry noticed two big silver cups on the
table and saw his judge whispering to the other judges.
They all looked at Ribsy. Ribsy panted harder than
ever. The judges had the winners show their dogs
again.

This time Henry wasn't taking any chances with the clothesline getting wound around his legs. He wound it around his hand so that there was only a foot of rope between his hand and Ribsy's collar. Ribsy did not behave any better the second time he was shown than he had the first. When Henry's turn came to lead him across the ring, he stopped to growl at a boxer. The boxer growled back.

Henry heard Scooter say, "If that mutt doesn't look out, he's going to get all bit up."

Ribsy growled louder. The snarling boxer advanced, dragging the little girl who owned him along on the end of his leash.

Henry tried to pull Ribsy away but Ribsy ignored him. The dogs circled around one another, pulling their owners after them. Henry yanked so hard at Ribsy's collar the dog choked. The boxer snarled and sprang at Ribsy, using his powerful front paws to knock over the smaller dog. Henry's hand was wound in the rope and he could not let go. He was pulled down on his stomach with his face in the grass.

"Look! Henry's in a dog fight!" screamed Beezus in great excitement.

The boxer's owner began to cry.

Henry was so mixed up he wasn't sure what was happening. He smelled the damp grass and felt it tickling his nose. He could hear snarls, growls, and barks. He could hear children screaming and yelling. The boxer stepped on his back. Henry said, "Oof!" He lifted his face from the grass in time to see a boy scout try to stop the fight by throwing a pan of water at the dogs. He missed the dogs but he didn't miss Henry.

Two judges ran into the ring and grabbed the dogs by their hind legs. They yanked the snarling animals apart.

"All right, son. Go ahead," ordered one judge, while the other helped the little girl hold her boxer.

Embarrassed and dripping, Henry got up from the grass and, without looking either right or left, hurried Ribsy across the ring and back.

Finally only Henry and another boy were left. The judge stepped to the center of the ring. "The big cup for the best dog in the whole show goes to the boy with the setter." Everybody clapped when he handed the boy one of the big silver cups. Ribsy growled at the winner.

105

"And now," said the judge, "the cup for the most unusual dog in the show goes to the boy with the a—a—mixed-breed dog!" He handed Henry the other big silver cup.

"Gee, thanks," was all Henry could say. The audience clapped and he heard Beezus shout, "Hooray for Henry!" He thought Ribsy looked pleased.

Everyone gathered around to admire his cup until a newspaper photographer asked them to stand back while he took a picture of Henry and his dog and wrote down his name and address. Henry was going to have his picture in the paper!

"Congratulations," said Scooter, "but I still think he's a mutt."

"Well, anyway, he won a bigger cup than Rags," boasted Henry, "but I guess Rags is a pretty good dog, too. Good old Ribsy. Now we'll get you a drink of water."

He led Ribsy to the nearest drinking fountain. He filled the silver cup with water and put it on the ground. Ribsy greedily lapped the water. Henry patted him. "Good old Ribsy. I knew you wouldn't drink out of any dish but your own."

The Young Puppy

by

A. A. MILNE

There was a young puppy called Howard,
Who at fighting was rather a coward.
    He never quite ran
    When the battle began,
But he started at once to bow-wow hard.

The Diners in the Kitchen

by

JAMES WHITCOMB RILEY

 Our dog Fred
Ate the bread.

Our dog Dash
Ate the hash.

 Our dog Pete
Ate the meat.

Our dog Davy
Ate the gravy.

Our dog Toffy
Ate the coffee.

Our dog Jake
Ate the cake.

Our dog Trip
Ate the dip.

And—the worst,
From the first,—

Our dog Fido
Ate the pie dough.

Pecos Bill and His Pony

from a story by

ANNE BURNETT MALCOLMSON

This tale about Pecos Bill and his pony is from the story "Pecos Bill and His Bouncing Bride." You can read more about the adventures of Pecos Bill in Anne Malcolmson's book *Yankee Doodle's Cousins.*

ecos Bill loved his horse, Widow-Maker, a beautiful creamy white mustang.

Widow-Maker was the wildest pony in the West. He was the son of the White Mustang. Like his father he had a proud spirit which refused to be broken. For many years cowboys and *vaqueros* had tried to capture him.

At last Pecos Bill succeeded. He had a terrible time of it. For a whole week he lay beside a water hole before he could lasso the white pony. For another week he had to ride across the prairies, in and out of canyons and briar patches, before he could bring the pony to a walk. It was a wild ride indeed. But after Bill's ride on the cyclone it was nothing.

111

At last the white stallion gave up the struggle. Pecos patted his neck gently and spoke to him in horse language. "I hope you will not be offended," he began as politely as possible, "but beauty such as yours is rare, even in this glorious state of Texas. I have no wish to break your proud spirit. I feel that together you and I would make a perfect team. Will you not be my partner at the I.X.L. Ranch?"

The horse neighed sadly. "It must be," he sighed. "I must give up my freedom. But since I must, I am glad that you are the man who has conquered me. Only Pecos Bill is worthy to fix a saddle upon the son of the great White Stallion, the Ghost King of the Prairie."

"I am deeply honored," said Pecos Bill, touched in his heart by the compliment.

"It is rather myself who am honored," replied the mustang, taking a brighter view of the situation.

The two of them went on for several hours saying nice things to each other. Before they were through, the pony was begging Pecos to be his master. Pecos was weeping and saying he was not fit to ride so magnificent a beast. In the end, however, Pecos Bill made two solemn promises. He would never place a bit in the pony's mouth. No other human would ever sit in his saddle.

When Bill rode back to I.X.L. with his new mount, the second promise was broken. Old Satan, the former bad man, had not completely recovered from his badness. He was jealous of Bill. When he saw the beautiful white stallion he turned green and almost burst with jealousy. One night he stole out to the corral. Quietly he slipped up beside the horse and jumped into the saddle.

Pegasus, as the horse was called, knew that his rider was not Pecos Bill. He lifted his four feet off the ground and bent his back into a perfect semicircle. Old Satan flew off like an arrow from a bow.

113

He flew up into the air, above the moon, and came down with a thud on top of Pike's Peak. There he sat howling with pain and fright until the boys at I.X.L. spotted him.

Bill was angry. He knew, however, that Old Satan had had enough punishment. In his kind heart he could not allow the villain to suffer any more than he had to. So he twirled his lasso around his head, let it fly, and roped Old Satan back to the Texas ranch. The former desperado never tried to be bad again.

The cowhands were so impressed by the pony's bucking they decided to change his name. From that time on they dropped the name of Pegasus and called him Widow-Maker. It suited him better.

Yarns

from

THE PEOPLE, YES

by

CARL SANDBURG

They have yarns
   of a skyscraper so tall
      they had to put hinges
         on the two top stories
            so to let the moon go by. . . .

Of Pecos Pete straddling a cyclone
   in Texas and riding it to the west coast. . . .

Of Paul Bunyan's big blue ox, Babe,
   measuring between the eyes
      forty-two handles. . . .

Of John Henry's hammer
   and the curve of its swing
      and his singing of it
         as "a rainbow round my shoulder". . .

They have yarns. . . .

Abe Lincoln and His Books

from

ABE LINCOLN GROWS UP

by

CARL SANDBURG

he farm boys talked about how Abe Lincoln was always reading. He was always digging into books, stretched out flat on his stomach in front of the fireplace.

This big boy of the backwoods wanted to learn. He wanted to know, to live, to reach out, and some of what he wanted so much, so deep down, seemed to be in books. He told people, "My best friend is the man who'll git me a book I ain't read."

John Hanks worked in the fields barefooted beside Abe, and John liked to tell stories about Abe and his books.

"When Abe and I came back to the house from work, he'd go to the kitchen, grab a piece of corn bread, sit down, and reach for his book," said John.

"Then he'd cock his legs up, high as his head, and read. Whenever Abe had a chance, he would sit and read, and sometimes, when he was spoken to, no answer came from him. He was far away, into the book."

Abe Lincoln liked to explain to other people what he was getting from books. Explaining an idea to someone else made it clearer to him. Also, he liked to read out loud. Words became more real if picked from the page of the book and spoken out loud.

When writing letters for his father, he read the words out loud as they got written. Before writing a letter for a friend, he would ask a lot of questions. "What do you want to say in the letter? How do you want to say it? Are you sure that's the best way to say it or do you think we can fix up a better way to say it?"

Besides reading the family Bible, Abe got hold of *Aesop's Fables.* The fables sank deep in his mind. He read through the book a second and third time, and the lessons of the fables stayed much in his thoughts.

He was thankful to the writer of *Aesop's Fables.* That writer gave him different things to think about, when most of his life was the same thing, day after day, over and over again.

So many mornings, he carried the same pails to draw water from the same spring. There was always the same corn bread to eat. He did the same field work and had the same tired feeling at the end of each day. So many days he was alone in the fields, or else he had the same people to talk with, people who always said the same things.

Yet there ran through his head the stories and sayings of other people, the stories and sayings of writers, the learnings his eyes had caught from books. They were good to have because they were good by themselves, and they were still better to have because they lit the dark rooms of his lonely hours.

Well—maybe the time would come when he would be free from work for a few weeks, or a few months, with books, and then he would read. Yes, then he would read. Then he would go and get at the proud secrets of his books.

William Tell, the Apple, and the Arrows

from

AROUND THE WORLD STORY BOOK

by

DANNY KAYE

n Switzerland long ago, there was a hunter named William Tell. He was a large man, proud and strong, who always carried his crossbow. He was so good a marksman that he could bring down a running rabbit with one arrow. William Tell was also a kind man who loved his family and prized his freedom.

But he and his countrymen had lost much of their freedom to the Austrian soldiers. Times were bad for the people of Switzerland.

Their Austrian governor, Gessler, was a hard man. He had his soldiers kill many who would not do as he ordered. The people hated him. Sometimes he ordered them to do silly things, just to make them feel small and helpless. One time, he ordered the people to bow down to a hat that he set up on a pole in the town square.

When William Tell came to the square with his young son Walter, he walked by the hat without bowing, so the governor's soldiers grabbed him. They took away his crossbow and arrows, and they brought him before Gessler.

"I am your governor, William Tell," said Gessler, "so you must do as I order, like it or not. Now, bow down to me, and tell me that from now on you will bow down to the hat on the pole, or to whatever I wish."

William Tell stood tall. He looked the governor straight in the eye. But he did not bow, and he said not a word.

His little son Walter stood in front of the people who were watching. "I won't bow either," he called out. "I am William Tell's son."

The governor looked down at him. "Oh, Tell's son, are you? I should have guessed. A little mouse who won't take orders. Like father, like son."

Gessler turned back to William Tell. "This is your last chance. Bow before me, and say in front of all these countrymen of yours that I am your ruler, just and true."

William Tell held his head high. He looked daggers at Gessler, but he did not speak.

"You are a fool," Gessler shouted. "Since you will not speak now, I shall see to it that you never speak again." With a wave of his hand, Gessler turned to one of his soldiers. "Let the people see what happens to such a man. Run him through."

The soldier raised his spear.

William Tell stood without flinching.

"Stop," Gessler ordered, watching William Tell in surprise. The soldier lowered his spear. "This man is not afraid to die," Gessler went on. "We will have to think of something else." The governor looked at William Tell thoughtfully.

Walter ran to his father's side, and he slipped his hand into his father's.

Gessler smiled a hard smile. "I have heard that you are a great bowman, William Tell. I have heard that you are a better shot than my soldiers. Is that true?"

"I do not know how well your soldiers shoot," said Tell.

"He is the best," yelled a voice from the town square, and others joined in, shouting for William Tell.

"Ah, so your friends think well of you," Gessler said.

123

"Well, we will give them a little show. This is how we will do it. Your son shall be placed over a hundred yards from you, off in the far corner of this square."

The governor rubbed his hands together and went on. "We will put an apple on his head—a fine, big, red apple—and you will shoot it off with one arrow."

"No!" cried William Tell. "I will not do it."

"Yes, you will," said Gessler. "It is my order. If you try to walk away from this test, you shall see your son killed before your eyes. If you miss and hurt your son, we will hang you for the killing of a child. But if you shoot the apple cleanly, I will let both you and your son go free."

William Tell stepped back. "You cannot ask this of me! Kill me, if you will, but let my boy go home."

Gessler laughed. "Your voice is shaking, William Tell. Keep cool, or your hands will shake as you shoot the arrow."

"Father," Walter said, tugging at his father's hand, "I am not afraid. You can do it. You always bring down a running rabbit with one shot, and I will stand ever so still. I won't flinch."

125

Keeping his eyes on Walter, William Tell let himself be led to the near corner of the town square. A soldier grabbed Walter, walked him to the far corner, and tied him to a tree. Another soldier handed William Tell his crossbow and an arrow.

The people of the town pressed close, but the soldiers pushed them back with spears. A woman started crying.

"Quiet!" shouted Gessler. "Stand quiet. For too long I have heard talk of the great William Tell, the marksman of Switzerland! Now we will see what he can do."

A soldier placed an apple on Walter's head.

"Cover the child's eyes," Gessler yelled to his soldier.

"I don't need my eyes covered," called Walter. "My father will not miss. I am not afraid when he holds the bow."

"The child is brave, I must say," Gessler whispered to a soldier beside him, "but I will frighten him yet." He called to the boy, "Have you any last words to say to your father before he shoots at you?"

"Yes," shouted Walter. "Father, after you split the apple in half with your arrow, you and I will eat the two pieces."

Cheers went up from the people in the square. They laughed and clapped.

"No more talk!" yelled Gessler. "Get on with it!"

The people of the town grew quiet.

William Tell shook his head and rubbed one hand over his eyes. He looked at the arrow in his hand as if it were something strange that he had never seen before.

His son Walter stood as still as the tree trunk behind him.

William Tell looked at the boy, then at Gessler. He felt the point of his arrow and it broke under his thumb. "Bring me all my arrows," he said. "Let me choose the one I will use."

A soldier lined up William Tell's arrows on the ground before him. Tell picked up one arrow, shook his head, and put it down again. He held another in his hand and turned it over, but then he threw it to the side.

The next arrow seemed to please him. As he chose it for his crossbow, he slipped another into his belt. A soldier cleared away the arrows on the ground.

William Tell raised the crossbow to his shoulder.

He sighted on the apple set on his son's head. No foot moved. No one seemed to breathe.

William Tell stood looking at his son. His eyes were glassy. Then suddenly he drew the bow and shot. The arrow flew through the air. It split the apple and stuck in the tree behind Walter.

An uproar of shouting and cheering broke forth from the people. William Tell dropped to one knee. A soldier untied Walter, and the boy grabbed up the pieces of the apple and ran to his father.

"See, Father," he said, jumping up and down in front of him. "You did it. I knew you could."

Tell got to his feet and kissed his son. As he rose, he didn't notice that the second arrow fell from his belt to the ground.

But Gessler saw it at once. "Well, William Tell," he said, "you are indeed a bowman. But tell me, what of that second arrow, there, on the ground? Why did you hide it in your belt?"

William Tell started to answer. Then he stopped himself and stared at the ground.

"Come now," said Gessler. "I want to know. You have my word that you and your son will go free, but tell me why you hid a second arrow."

William Tell looked up. The color was coming back into his face. "The second arrow, Governor, was for you, if I had hit my son. I would not have missed your heart."

William Tell, Calvin and Hobbes

by

BILL WATTERSON

Calvin & Hobbes
© 1989 Universal Press Syndicate. Reprinted with permission.
All rights reserved.

Robin Hood at the Archers' Contest

A PLAY

adapted from an English legend

Robin Hood and His Merry Men
N. C. Wyeth
1917

Characters

Maid Marian
Lady Ellen
Friar Tuck
Little John
Robin Hood (wearing
    a cook's apron and
    a black patch over
    one eye)
The Sheriff of
    Nottingham

Maid Marian

Setting

The story takes place long ago in England at an
archers' contest near Sherwood Forest. All six of
the characters are at the contest. The Sheriff
stands alone. The other three men are in a
group to the side. Maid Marian and Lady Ellen
are talking.

Maid Marian   I'm worried about Robin Hood. I
heard that the Sheriff is planning to capture
him at this archers' meet.

133

Lady Ellen   Don't worry, Maid Marian. I was just talking with Friar Tuck and some of Robin Hood's other men. They found out about the Sheriff's plan, so Friar Tuck has already told Robin Hood not to come to this meet.

Maid Marian   I wonder if Robin Hood will listen to the good Friar. You know how he loves to show his skill with the bow and arrow. He would love to win the prize.

Lady Ellen   But he might not win today. It's true that Robin Hood is the best archer in Sherwood Forest, but some of the best archers in all of England will be in today's shooting meet.

Maid Marian   That is all the more reason why Robin Hood will come, even though Friar Tuck told him not to. I'm worried.

Lady Ellen   Well, I see a sight that will stop you from worrying and make you laugh. Look at the man in the cook's apron who is getting in line to shoot. What a clown!

Maid Marian   Where?

Lady Ellen   Over there, near Friar Tuck and Little John.

Maid Marian   Oh, yes, now I see him. But he looks more like a pirate than a cook, with that black patch on his eye.

Lady Ellen   See how Friar Tuck and Little John are pointing at him and laughing.

Maid Marian   The Sheriff has noticed him too, I see. Maybe he means to throw the stranger out of line. He wouldn't take kindly to a cook with an eye patch making a joke of his archers' contest.

Lady Ellen

Lady Ellen   Let's walk over and hear what Friar Tuck is saying to the stranger.

      (Exit)

135

Friar Tuck   My good man, do you really mean to shoot with a patch over one eye? Even with both my eyes, I did not shoot well today.

Little John (whispering to the man with the black patch over his eye)   Friar Tuck may pretend not to know you, but he really knows who you are as well as I do. It is you, Robin Hood, hiding behind that eye patch and that cook's apron.

Robin Hood   I can't fool the two of you, but I hope to fool others here.

Friar Tuck   May you fool the Sheriff! You know that he hopes to trap you at this contest. You should not have come, Robin. I told you.

Robin Hood   Indeed you did, but you knew I wouldn't listen. The Sheriff is a fool. I have tricked him before, and I will trick him again today.

Little John   Well, we won't give you away, not to the Sheriff and not even to the two young ladies coming this way.

Robin Hood   Oh, it's Maid Marian, with Lady Ellen.

(The ladies approach the group.)

Little John   And the Sheriff is joining us too. Good day to you, Sheriff.

Sheriff   So, Little John of Sherwood Forest! I see you are here, trying your skill, though I don't know why. No archer from Sherwood Forest could be good enough to win this contest.

Little John   What about Robin Hood?

Sheriff   Ah, yes. Robin Hood. Where is your friend Robin Hood?

Little John   Am I my friend's keeper? How am I to know where Robin Hood might be?

Sheriff   Come now, he can't stay away from a shooting meet. Before the day is over, he will walk right into my hands.

Maid Marian   Robin Hood is too clever for that, Sheriff. I don't think he'll come to this meet. He knows that *you* will be handing the prize to the winner. And, of course, he would win.

Sheriff   No, he would not win this meet. My new archer, Giles of the Green Valley, is here today.

Lady Ellen   Giles of the Green Valley? I've heard of him. His skill is supposed to be so great that archers from far and near are afraid to shoot against him.

Sheriff   And people come from miles around to watch him. That stranger in the cook's apron must be here just to see Giles shoot. Giles of the Green Valley is a far better shot than Robin Hood.

Friar Tuck   Not so! There's not an archer in England who is a better shot than Robin Hood.

Sheriff   Just watch Giles of the Green Valley. He is taking his place to shoot now.

Little John   He's slow about it. He's still fitting his arrow to the bow.

Robin Hood   But look at his arms. He has sent many an arrow flying far and fast.

Friar Tuck

Sheriff I'm for you, Giles. Take your time. Shoot straight and true now. There! His arrow landed just a hand away from the middle of the mark.

Friar Tuck A fair hit, I must say.

Little John Better than I thought he would do.

Robin Hood A good shot! A fine shot! Giles of the Green Valley should try his luck in Sherwood Forest. He might be welcomed by Robin Hood himself.

Sheriff What! Watch your words, stranger. Welcomed indeed! No archer of mine will ever be anything but an enemy to Robin Hood.

Robin Hood Tell me more about this man you call Robin Hood. Is he a good archer?

Sheriff Not as good as he thinks he is. Not as good as Giles of the Green Valley.

Robin Hood I wonder if Robin Hood is as good a shot as I am.

Sheriff   You? Why, stranger, look at you! You are dressed like a cook, not an archer, and you have a patch over one eye. There is no way you could see well enough to hit the mark.

Robin Hood   But I still wish to try my skill in your contest. Maybe I will win the silver arrow.

Sheriff   I have no time for the likes of you. I must keep on the lookout for Robin Hood.

Maid Marian   If Robin Hood were here, do you think he would let you see him?

Sheriff   How could he help it? If he means to shoot in my contest, he must show himself here. And he always wears green clothing and heavy boots, so he will be easy to spot.

Lady Ellen   Certainly Robin Hood knows better than to show his face here. He won't come to your meet.

Sheriff   Then I will be able to say he was afraid to come, afraid to face me, knowing I'd capture him, and afraid to shoot against Giles of the Green Valley.

Little John   Robin Hood has never in his life been afraid of any archer, or any sheriff.

Friar Tuck   It is getting late. If Robin had meant to come at all, he would be here by now.

Sheriff   Maybe yes and maybe no. He is tricky.

Maid Marian   He is the best archer in England. If he comes late, even if he is the last to shoot, he will still win the silver arrow.

Little John

Little John   That is true. The meet is not over yet. Robin Hood may still have a turn. But while we are waiting, let's see how well the one-eyed cook shoots.

Sheriff   No. No shots from strangers in aprons and eye patches. I won't have any clowning around in this contest.

Robin Hood   But I'm not clowning around. Won't you give a stranger a chance?

Sheriff   Stop being silly, stranger. Put down your bow, and hold this silver arrow for me while I call the archers together.

Robin Hood (putting the silver arrow in his pocket) Wait! Just let me have time for one shot.

Sheriff   I don't want to wait any longer to give the prize. It is time for me to name Giles of the Green Valley as the winner of the meet. No arrow has hit closer than his.

Robin Hood   You have not yet given me my turn.

Sheriff   Why do you keep acting the fool, stranger! You are making me angry! You know you can't shoot with a patch over one eye.

Robin Hood   Watch me. (He shoots. Then, as everyone watches the arrow, he quickly walks away.)

Little John   Look! The stranger's arrow hit right in the middle.

Robin Hood

142

Friar Tuck   A perfect shot!

Sheriff   A lucky hit, that's all. Just luck.

Little John   Not luck but skill.

Lady Ellen   Oh, to hit the middle of the mark!
What a shot!

Sheriff   With a patch over one eye, a man is lucky
to come close, let alone hit the middle. I must
take a closer look at his arrow.

Maid Marian   Lady Ellen and I will come with you
for that closer look, Sheriff, but I'm sure that you
gave the prize rightly. I saw you hand the silver
arrow to the man with the black patch on his
eye, whoever he may be.

Lady Ellen   I have never seen a finer shot than the
stranger made. Have you, Sheriff?

Sheriff   No, if it were made with skill and not with
luck. I want the stranger to shoot again. He will
never hit the mark a second time. Where is he?

Lady Ellen   I don't see him.

Sheriff   What was his name?

143

Maid Marian   He never said. But, then again, you never asked him, did you, Sheriff?

Sheriff   Where could he have gone? And where are Friar Tuck and Little John? They were talking with that stranger. I want them to help me find him.

Lady Ellen   Maybe they want to find him themselves. Maybe they want to take him back to Sherwood Forest with them. Remember, you told Little John that no archer from Sherwood Forest had the skill to win your contest.

Maid Marian   Very few archers have the skill to hit the middle of the mark. In these parts, only Robin Hood is said to have such skill.

Sheriff   But Robin Hood did not come to my contest.

Maid Marian   Are you sure, Sheriff? Are you quite sure that he has not been here?

Sheriff   I have not seen him. He did not show himself to me today. Why do you ask? Did you see him?

Maid Marian   I think I may have seen him. And I believe Robin Hood did show himself to you, even though you don't think you have seen him today.

Sheriff   How can this be?

Lady Ellen   Wait! I think I understand. Maid Marian, are you saying that the stranger might have been none other than Robin Hood himself, hiding behind a cook's apron?

Sheriff   No! It couldn't be that he tricked me so! I don't believe it.

Maid Marian   We will soon know for sure. Look at the stranger's arrow. See the bit of paper on the end of it. I think the archer in the cook's apron left a message. Read it to us, Sheriff.

Sheriff   "No stranger walked away with your prize, Sheriff. No one-eyed cook made a joke of your contest. An archer from Sherwood Forest won the silver arrow, an archer that you know well, an archer named Robin Hood."

Sheriff

145

The Arrow and the Song

by

HENRY WADSWORTH LONGFELLOW

I shot an arrow into the air.
It fell to earth, I knew not where.
So swift it flew that no one's sight
Could ever follow in its flight.

I breathed a song into the air.
It fell to earth, I knew not where.
For who has sight so keen and strong
That it can follow the flight of song?

Long, long afterwards, in an oak
I found the arrow, still unbroke.
And the song, from beginning to end,
I found again in the heart of a friend.

147

Chums

by

BUSON

A shower in spring,
And there in lively talk,
A rain coat and umbrella walk!

Damon and Pythias

a Greek legend of friendship

ong ago in Greece lived a cruel king whose heart was as hard as stone. He was cruel to his own people, but he was even crueler to people from other countries who visited his land.

A fine young man named Pythias once traveled to this land with his good friend Damon. Even though Pythias had done no wrong, he was taken prisoner by the king.

"Pythias must die. It is my will," said the king.

Damon went down on his knees before the king, begging for his friend's life, but in this land the king's word was the last word. Nobody could move him, and nobody could stand up against him.

Pythias knew there was no hope, but still he cried out, "If only I could see my wife and my baby once more before I die."

He threw himself down before the king.

149

"Give me one month," he begged. "Let me return to my homeland and say good-bye to my family, and then I will return here—to die."

"You will return?" said the king, laughing. "Why should I believe you? What reason would there be for you to return?"

Damon stepped forward and said, "I will stay in place of Pythias. Let him go. If he does not return, I will give up my life in his place."

The king looked at Damon in surprise. He could hardly believe what he was hearing. Why should any man be willing to give his life for another? It was more than he could understand.

"You are a fool," he said to Damon. "Your friend Pythias will never return to save you."

"I will return," said Pythias. "I swear it! I swear by my friendship with Damon that in one month I will be back."

"Do you really believe he will return?" the king asked Damon.

"He swears by our friendship that he will be back," said Damon. "There is no stronger promise."

The king shook his head. He looked from Damon to Pythias and back.

"I will agree to the plan," he said slowly, "but I still do not believe that you mean to return, Pythias.

"You have one month," said the king. "If you are not here in one month exactly, Damon will die. And as for you, Damon, I still think you are a fool to be changing places with your friend. But since your life means so little to you, it doesn't matter if you lose your head anyway."

So Pythias was set free.

He returned to his land and told what had happened. It was the saddest of homecomings for Pythias.

"Do not go back," his wife begged.

"Stay here," said one friend after another.

But he would not listen to any of them. "Are you telling me to let my friend Damon die in my place?" he cried. "Would you have me be as cruel as the king himself? I must return."

Sadly he took leave of his family and friends, and he set out to return, on board a sailing ship.

But the winds were not friendly. They blew his ship off course, and Pythias found himself still at sea, days after he had planned to be on land. His fears for his friend Damon grew with every passing hour.

But Damon felt no fear. From the start, he had hoped he might die for his friend. "Pythias has a wife," thought Damon, "and he has a baby. His family loves him and needs him, and I have no family. It would be better if he were somehow kept from returning here. I will not be missed the way he would be missed."

When only one day was left before the end of the month, the king visited Damon. "Where is your friend?" he asked. "You see, he has forgotten you. He never meant to return."

"Pythias will return if he can," said Damon, "and if he cannot, I will die in his place."

"Yes, you will," said the king, with a cruel laugh, "so you had better make yourself ready to die tomorrow. I have given orders. Many of my people will be waiting to see the show. Tomorrow, you are to be led outside. There, your head will be cut off— unless your friend returns at the last minute to save you."

The next morning was bright and clear. As Damon was led out into the sunshine, he felt that it was a day to live, not a day to die. His hands were tied behind him, but he held himself tall and straight and he showed no fear, even when he was told to put his head on the block.

The king watched with a hard smile on his face. "Now!" he said.

Just then there was a cry from far down the road. "Stop!"

A rider on horseback was tearing toward the king. The people turned to see who was galloping so fast, racing against time.

A cry of surprise broke from the king. "Pythias!" he exclaimed.

And Pythias jumped down from his horse and ran to the block to take Damon's place.

153

"Hold!" shouted the king. "No heads will roll today."

He pulled Damon and Pythias to their feet. "Never before have I seen so strong a friendship! Would that I could have such a friend, or be such a friend. It is my will that both of you should live, and that now and forever, when the word *friendship* is used, the names Damon and Pythias will be remembered."

The Goose That Laid
the Golden Egg

from

AESOP'S FABLES

here was once a man who owned a
wonderful goose. Time and again, this wonderful
goose would lay just one egg. But it was always a
golden egg. Time and again, the man would sell
the golden egg. Then, right away, he would spend
all the money that he got for the egg.

The man bought fine clothes for himself,
and he bought silver dishes for his table. He grew
richer and richer, but the more he bought, the more
he wanted.

One day he said to his goose, "I am tired of
selling just one golden egg at a time. One is not
enough. I think you should lay two or three at a
time, or, better still, give me ten golden eggs at once.
Then I will be able to get enough money to buy
everything I want."

The goose said nothing. She just went on laying
one golden egg at a time.

Again and again the man told the goose that she must do better, but nothing he said seemed to matter. The goose did not change her ways.

Then the man got very angry. "I want more!" he shouted at the goose. "Your eggs bring me only a trickle of riches, little by little, and life is too short for me to wait for anything. I must buy all that I want right now! If you will not do things my way, you will be sorry."

Still the goose kept on as before.

At that point the man made up his mind. He would have all his riches at once. He would kill the goose and cut her open!

So he did. But what did he find inside when he cut her open? Instead of finding a pile of golden eggs, he found that she was just like any other goose. Now he had nothing left but a goose that could be cooked and eaten.

The man held his head in his hands. "If only I had been happy with one golden egg at a time! My trickle of riches would have added up, little by little. In time, I could have bought everything I wanted," he moaned.

**It does not pay to kill the goose
that lays the golden egg.**

157

El perro y el cocodrilo

de

FÉLIX MARÍA DE SAMANIEGO

Bebiendo un perro en el Nilo,
al mismo tiempo corría.
—Bebe quieto—le decía
un taimado cocodrilo.

Díjole el perro prudente:
—Dañoso es beber y andar,
pero ¿es sano el aguardar
a que me claves el diente?

¡Oh, qué docto perro viejo!
Yo venero tu sentir
en esto de no seguir
del enemigo el consejo.

The Dog and the Crocodile

by

FÉLIX MARÍA DE SAMANIEGO

A dog, while drinking from the Nile,
Was running at the same time.
"Drink without moving about," said to him
A sly crocodile.

The prudent dog said to him:
"It may be harmful to drink and walk,
But is it healthy to wait
Until you sink your teeth in me?"

Oh, what a wise old dog!
I respect your judgment
In this matter of not following
The advice of an enemy.

159

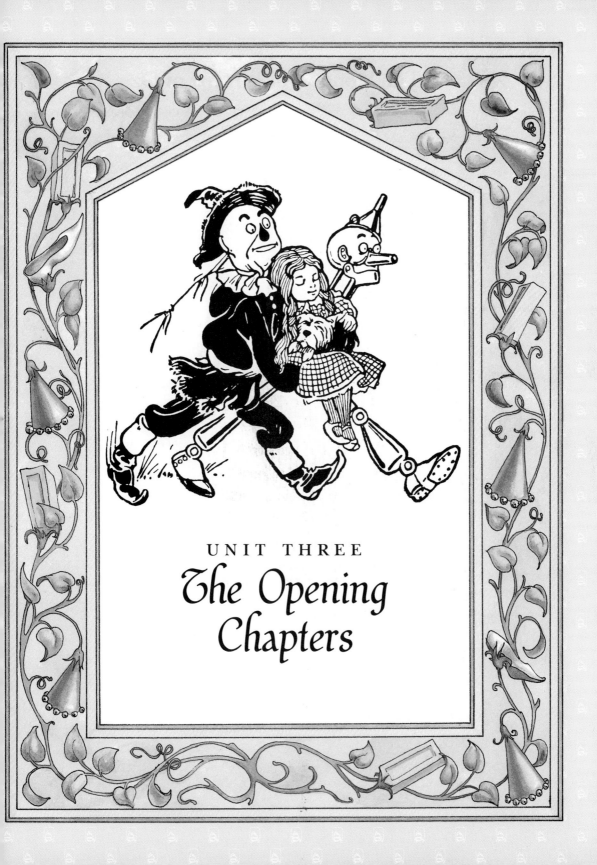

UNIT THREE
The Opening Chapters

The Wonderful Wizard of Oz

by

L. FRANK BAUM

CHAPTER ONE
The Cyclone

Dorothy and her little dog, Toto, lived in Kansas with her Uncle Henry and Aunt Em. The house was very small and flat, with no upstairs rooms.

There was no real cellar, either. There was just a small hole, dug in the ground, called a cyclone cellar. This tiny cyclone cellar was reached by a trap door in the middle of the floor, from which a ladder led down into the small dark hole.

Today Uncle Henry was sitting on the doorstep watching the sky. Suddenly he stood up and said, "There's a cyclone coming!"

He ran out to take care of the farm animals. Aunt Em dropped her work and went to the door. One look at the sky told her danger was close at hand.

"Quick, Dorothy!" she screamed. "Run for the cellar!"

But Toto jumped from Dorothy's arms and hid under the bed. As Dorothy reached for Toto, a strange thing happened. A gust of wind lifted the house and whirled it around two or three times.

The house rose slowly through the air. It was carried miles and miles away.

Hour after hour passed, and slowly Dorothy got over her fright. At last she crawled over the swaying floor to her bed and lay down upon it. Toto followed and lay down beside her.

In spite of the swaying of the house and the wailing of the wind, Dorothy soon closed her eyes and fell fast asleep.

CHAPTER TWO
The Council with the Munchkins

She was awakened by a jolt, so hard
and sudden that if she had not been lying on the soft
bed Dorothy might have been hurt. As it was, the jolt
made her catch her breath and wonder what had
happened.

Toto put his cold little nose into her face and
whined. Dorothy sat up and noticed that the house
was not moving, nor was it dark, for the bright
sunshine came in at the window. She jumped up from
her bed. Then, with Toto at her heels, she ran and
opened the door.

The girl gave a cry of surprise as she looked about.

The cyclone had set her house down, very gently—for a cyclone—in a country of great beauty. There were green fields all around, with trees bearing rich fruits. Banks of flowers were on all sides, and birds sang in the bushes. A little way off was a small stream, rushing between green banks.

While Dorothy stood looking at all the strange sights, she saw coming toward her a group of strange-looking people. They were not as big as the grown-ups she had always been used to, but neither were they very small. They seemed to be about as tall as Dorothy, though they were many years older.

Three were men and one was a woman. All were strangely dressed. The men wore round hats that rose to a small point a foot above their heads, with little bells around the brims that jingled as they moved. They were about as old as Uncle Henry, Dorothy thought, for two of them had beards. The woman's hair was nearly white. She too wore a pointed hat and a long white gown that had sparkling stars all over it.

The little woman walked up to Dorothy and made a low bow.

"Welcome, great Sorceress, to the Land of the Munchkins," she said in a sweet voice. "We are grateful to you for killing the Wicked Witch of the East and for setting the Munchkins free."

Dorothy listened to this speech with wonder. What could the little woman mean by calling her a sorceress? And how could the woman say that she had killed the Wicked Witch of the East? Dorothy was a harmless little girl, who had been carried far from home by a cyclone. She had never killed anything in all her life.

But the little woman seemed to be waiting for her to answer. So Dorothy said, "You are very kind. But there must be some mistake. I have not killed anything."

"Your house did anyway," said the little old woman, with a sweet laugh. "And that is the same thing. See!" she went on, pointing to the corner of the house. "There are the witch's feet, still sticking out from under a block of wood."

Dorothy looked, and gave a little cry of fright. There, indeed, sticking out from just under the corner of the house, were two feet wearing silver shoes with pointed toes.

"Oh, dear! Oh, dear!" cried Dorothy. "The house must have fallen on her. Whatever shall we do?"

"There is nothing to be done," said the little woman.

"But who was she?" asked Dorothy.

"She was the Wicked Witch of the East, as I said," answered the little woman. "For many years she has made the Munchkins slave for her, day and night. Now they are all set free, and they are very grateful to you."

"Who are the Munchkins?" asked Dorothy.

"They are the people who live in this land."

"Are you a Munchkin?" Dorothy asked the woman.

"No, but I am their friend, though I live in the land of the North. When they saw that the Wicked Witch of the East was dead, they sent for me. I came at once. I am the Witch of the North."

"Oh," cried Dorothy. "Are you a real witch?"

"Yes, indeed," answered the little woman. "But I am a good witch, and the people love me. I am not as powerful as the Wicked Witch was who ruled here, or I should have set the people free myself."

"But I thought all witches were wicked," said the girl.

"Oh, no, that is a great mistake. There were only four witches in all the Land of Oz, and two of them, those who live in the North and the South, are good witches. I know this is true, for I am one of them myself, and cannot be mistaken. Those who dwelt in the East and the West were, indeed, wicked witches. But now that you have killed one of them, there is but one Wicked Witch in all the Land of Oz—the one who lives in the West."

"But," said Dorothy, after a moment's thought, "Aunt Em has told me that the witches were all dead—years and years ago."

"Who is Aunt Em?" inquired the little old woman.

"She is my aunt who lives in Kansas, where I came from."

The Witch of the North seemed to think for a time, with her head bowed and her eyes upon the ground. Then she looked up and said, "I do not know where Kansas is, for I have never heard that country mentioned before. But tell me, is it a civilized country?"

"Oh, yes," replied Dorothy.

"Then that accounts for it. In the civilized countries I believe there are no witches left, nor wizards, nor sorceresses, nor magicians. But, you see, the Land of Oz has never been civilized, for we are cut off from the rest of the world. Therefore we still have witches and wizards amongst us."

"Who are the wizards?" asked Dorothy.

"Oz himself is the Great Wizard," answered the Witch, sinking her voice to a whisper. "He is more powerful than all the rest of us together. He lives in the City of Emeralds."

Dorothy was going to ask another question. But just then the Munchkins, who had been standing silently by, gave a loud shout and pointed to the corner of the house where the Wicked Witch had been lying.

"What is it?" asked the little old woman and looked, and began to laugh. The feet of the dead Witch had disappeared. Nothing was left but the silver shoes.

"She was so old," explained the Witch of the North, "that she dried up quickly in the sun. That is the end of her. But the silver shoes are yours. And you shall have them to wear."

She reached down and picked up the shoes, and after shaking the dust out of them handed them to Dorothy.

"The Witch of the East was proud of those silver shoes," said one of the Munchkins. "There is some charm connected with them. But what it is we never knew."

Dorothy carried the shoes into the house and placed them on the table. Then she came out again to the Munchkins and said, "I am anxious to get back to my aunt and uncle, for I am sure they will worry about me. Can you help me find my way?"

The Munchkins and the Witch first looked at one another, and then at Dorothy, and then shook their heads.

"At the East, not far from here," said one, "there is a great desert. None could live to cross it."

"It is the same at the South," said another, "for I have been there and seen it. The South is the country of the Quadlings."

"I am told," said the third man, "that it is the same at the West. And that country where the Winkies live is ruled by the Wicked Witch of the West. She would make you her slave if you passed her way."

"The North is my home," said the old lady. "At its edge is the same great desert that surrounds this Land of Oz. I'm afraid, my dear, you will have to live with us."

Dorothy began to sob at this, for she felt lonely among all these strange people. Her tears seemed to grieve the kind-hearted Munchkins, for they immediately took out their handkerchiefs and began to weep also. As for the little old woman, she took off her cap and balanced the point on the end of her nose. Then she counted "One, two, three" in a solemn voice. At once the cap changed to a slate, on which was written in big, white chalk marks:

LET DOROTHY GO TO THE CITY OF EMERALDS

The little old woman took the slate from her nose. Having read the words on it, she asked, "Is your name Dorothy, my dear?"

"Yes," answered the child, looking up.

"Then you must go to the City of Emeralds. Perhaps Oz will help you. The City is exactly in the center of the country, and is ruled by Oz, the Great Wizard I told you of."

"Is he a good man?" inquired the girl anxiously.

"He is a good Wizard. Whether he is a man or not I cannot tell, for I have never seen him."

"How can I get there?" asked Dorothy.

"You must walk. It is a long journey, through a country that is sometimes pleasant and sometimes dark and terrible. However, I will use all the magic arts I know of to keep you from harm."

"Won't you go with me?" pleaded the girl, who had begun to see the little old woman as her only friend.

"No, I cannot do that," she replied. "But I will give you my kiss. And no one will dare injure a person who has been kissed by the Witch of the North."

She came close to Dorothy and kissed her gently on the forehead. Where her lips touched the girl they left a round, shining mark, as Dorothy found out soon after.

"The road to the City of Emeralds is paved with yellow brick," said the Witch. "So you cannot miss it. When you get to Oz do not be afraid of him, but tell your story and ask him to help you. Good-bye, my dear."

The three Munchkins bowed low to her and wished her a pleasant journey, after which they walked away through the trees. The Witch gave Dorothy a friendly little nod, whirled around on her left heel three times, and straightway disappeared.

CHAPTER THREE

How Dorothy Saved the Scarecrow

When Dorothy was left alone she began to feel hungry. So she went to the cupboard and cut herself some bread, which she spread with butter. She gave some to Toto, and taking a pail from the shelf she carried it down to the little brook and filled it with clear, sparkling water. Toto ran over to the trees and began to bark at the birds sitting there.

Dorothy went to get him, and saw such delicious fruit hanging from the branches that she gathered some of it, finding it just what she wanted to help out her breakfast.

Then she went back to the house, and having helped herself and Toto to a good drink of the cool, clear water, she set about making ready for the journey to the City of Emeralds.

Dorothy had only one other dress. But that happened to be clean and was hanging on a peg beside her bed. It was gingham, with checks of white and blue. Though the blue was somewhat faded with many washings, it was still a pretty frock.

She washed herself carefully, dressed herself in the clean gingham, and tied her pink sunbonnet on her head. She took a little basket and filled it with bread from the cupboard, laying a white cloth over the top. Then she looked down at her feet and noticed how old and worn her shoes were.

"They surely will never do for a long journey, Toto," she said. And Toto looked up into her face with his little black eyes and wagged his tail to show he knew what she meant.

At that moment Dorothy saw lying on the table the silver shoes that had belonged to the Witch of the East.

"I wonder if they will fit me," she said to Toto. "They would be just the thing to take a long walk in, for they could not wear out."

She took off her old leather shoes and tried on the silver ones, which fitted her as well as if they had been made for her.

Finally she picked up her basket.

"Come along, Toto," she said. "We will go to the Emerald City and ask the great Oz how to get back to Kansas again."

She closed the door, locked it, and put the key carefully in the pocket of her dress. And so, with Toto trotting along behind her, she started on her journey.

There were several roads near by. But it did not take her long to find the one paved with yellow brick. Within a short time she was walking briskly toward the Emerald City, her silver shoes tinkling merrily on the hard, yellow roadbed.

The sun shone bright and the birds sang sweetly, and Dorothy did not feel nearly so bad as you might think a little girl would who had been suddenly whisked away from her own country and set down in the midst of a strange land.

She was surprised, as she walked along, to see how pretty the country was about her. There were neat fences at the sides of the road, painted a dainty blue color. Beyond them were fields of grain and vegetables in abundance. Evidently the Munchkins were good farmers and able to raise large crops.

Once in a while she would pass a house, and the people came out to look at her and bow low as she went by; for everyone knew she had been the means of destroying the Wicked Witch and setting them free from bondage. The houses of the Munchkins were odd-looking dwellings, for each was round, with a big dome for a roof. All were painted blue, for in this country of the East blue was the favorite color.

Towards evening, when Dorothy was tired with her long walk and began to wonder where she should pass the night, she came to a house rather larger than the rest. On the green lawn before it many men and women were dancing.

Five little fiddlers played as loudly as possible and the people were laughing and singing, while a big table nearby was loaded with delicious fruits and nuts, pies, and cakes, and many other good things to eat.

The people greeted Dorothy kindly, and invited her to supper and to pass the night with them; for this was the home of one of the richest Munchkins in the land, and his friends were gathered with him to celebrate their freedom from the bondage of the Wicked Witch.

Dorothy ate a hearty supper and was waited upon by the rich Munchkin himself, whose name was Boq. Then she sat down upon a settee and watched the people dance.

When Boq saw her silver shoes he said, "You must be a great sorceress."

"Why?" asked the girl.

"Because you wear silver shoes and have killed the Wicked Witch. Besides, you have white in your frock, and only witches and sorceresses wear white."

"My dress is blue and white checked," said Dorothy, smoothing out the wrinkles in it.

"It is kind of you to wear that," said Boq. "Blue is

the color of the Munchkins, and white is the witch color. So we know you are a friendly witch."

Dorothy did not know what to say to this, for all the people seemed to think her a witch, and she knew very well she was only an ordinary little girl who had come by the chance of a cyclone into a strange land.

When she had tired watching the dancing, Boq led her into the house, where he gave her a room with a pretty bed in it. The sheets were made of blue cloth, and Dorothy slept soundly in them till morning, with Toto curled up on the blue rug beside her.

She ate a hearty breakfast, and watched a wee Munchkin baby, who played with Toto and pulled his tail and crowed and laughed in a way that greatly amused Dorothy. Toto was a fine curiosity to all the people, for they had never seen a dog before.

"How far is it to the Emerald City?" the girl asked.

"I do not know," answered Boq gravely, "for I have never been there. It is better for people to keep away from Oz, unless they have business with him. But it is a long way to the Emerald City, and it will take you many days. The country here is rich and pleasant.

181

But you must pass through rough and dangerous places before you reach the end of your journey."

This worried Dorothy a little, but she knew that only the great Oz could help her get to Kansas again, so she bravely resolved not to turn back.

She bade her friends good-bye, and again started along the road of yellow brick. When she had gone several miles she thought she would stop to rest, and so climbed to the top of the fence beside the road and sat down. There was a great cornfield beyond the fence, and not far away she saw a Scarecrow placed high on a pole to keep the birds from the ripe corn.

Dorothy leaned her chin upon her hand and gazed thoughtfully at the Scarecrow. Its head was a small sack stuffed with straw, with eyes, nose, and mouth painted on it to represent a face. An old, pointed blue hat, that had belonged to some Munchkin, was perched on his head, and the rest of the figure was a blue suit of clothes, worn and faded. On the feet were some old boots with blue tops, such as every man wore in this country, and the figure was raised above the stalks of corn by means of the pole stuck up its back.

While Dorothy was looking earnestly into the queer, painted face of the Scarecrow, she was surprised to see one of the eyes slowly wink at her. She thought she must have been mistaken at first, for none of the scarecrows in Kansas ever wink.

But presently the figure nodded its head to her in a friendly way. Then she climbed down from the fence and walked up to it, while Toto ran around the pole and barked.

"Good day," said the Scarecrow, in a rather husky voice.

"Did you speak?" asked the girl, in wonder.

"Certainly," answered the Scarecrow. "How do you do?"

"I'm pretty well, thank you," replied Dorothy, politely. "How do you do?"

"I'm not feeling well," said the Scarecrow with a smile, "for it is very tedious being perched up here night and day to scare away crows."

"Can't you get down?" asked Dorothy.

"No, for this pole is stuck up my back. If you will please take away the pole I shall be greatly obliged to you."

Dorothy reached up both arms and lifted the figure off the pole, for, being stuffed with straw, it was quite light.

"Thank you very much," said the Scarecrow, when he had been set down on the ground. "I feel like a new man."

Dorothy was puzzled at this, for it sounded queer to hear a stuffed man speak, and to see him bow and walk along beside her.

"Who are you?" asked the Scarecrow when he had stretched himself and yawned. "And where are you going?"

"My name is Dorothy," said the girl, "and I am

going to the Emerald City, to ask the great Oz to send me back to Kansas."

"Where is the Emerald City?" he inquired. "And who is Oz?"

"Why, don't you know?" she returned, in surprise.

"No, indeed; I don't know anything. You see, I am stuffed, so I have no brains at all," he answered, sadly.

"Oh," said Dorothy, "I'm awfully sorry for you."

"Do you think," he asked, "if I go to the Emerald City with you, that Oz would give me some brains?"

"I cannot tell," she returned. "But you may come with me, if you like. If Oz will not give you any brains you will be no worse off than you are now."

"That is true," said the Scarecrow. "You see," he continued confidentially, "I don't mind my legs and arms and body being stuffed, because I cannot get hurt. If anyone treads on my toes or sticks a pin into me, it doesn't matter, for I can't feel it. But I do not want people to call me a fool, and if my head stays stuffed with straw instead of with brains, as yours is, how am I ever to know anything?"

"I understand how you feel," said the little girl, who was truly sorry for him. "If you will come with me I'll ask Oz to do all he can for you."

"Thank you," he answered gratefully.

They walked back to the road. Dorothy helped him over the fence, and they started along the path of yellow brick for the Emerald City.

Toto did not like this addition to the party, at first. He smelled around the stuffed man as if he suspected there might be a nest of rats in the straw, and he often growled in an unfriendly way at the Scarecrow.

"Don't mind Toto," said Dorothy, to her new friend. "He never bites."

"Oh, I'm not afraid," replied the Scarecrow. "He can't hurt the straw. Do let me carry that basket for you. I shall not mind it, for I can't get tired. I'll tell you a secret," he continued, as he walked along. "There is only one thing in the world I am afraid of."

"What is that?" asked Dorothy. "The Munchkin farmer who made you?"

"No," answered the Scarecrow. "It's a lighted match."

UNIT FOUR

Nature and Nonsense

Habits of the Hippopotamus

by

ARTHUR GUITERMAN

The hippopotamus is strong
    And huge of head and broad of bustle.
The limbs on which he rolls along
    Are big with hippopotomuscle.

He does not greatly care for sweets
    Like ice cream, apple pie, or custard,
But takes to flavor what he eats
    A little hippopotomustard.

The hippopotamus is true
    To all his principles, and just.
He always tries his best to do
    The things one hippopotomust.

He never rides in trucks or trams,
    In taxicabs or omnibuses,
And so keeps out of traffic jams
    And other hippopotomusses.

How the Rhinoceros Got His Skin

from

JUST SO STORIES

by

RUDYARD KIPLING

nce upon a time, on an island far away, there lived a Parsee boy. The Parsee boy had nothing but his hat and his knife and a cooking stove.

One day he took flour and water and sugar, and made himself one cake, which was two feet across and three feet thick. It was indeed a fine cake. He put it on the stove, and he baked it and he baked it until it was all done brown and smelled most wonderful.

But just as he was going to eat it, there came down to the beach a rhinoceros. The rhinoceros had a horn on his nose, two tiny eyes, and few manners.

In those days the rhinoceros's skin fitted him quite tightly. There were no loose spots in it anywhere. But he had no manners then, and he has no manners now, and he never will have any manners.

He said, "How!"

And the Parsee boy left that cake and climbed to the top of a tree.

The rhinoceros upset the stove with his nose, and the cake rolled on the sand. He spiked that cake on the horn of his nose. He ate it, and he went away, waving his tail.

The Parsee boy came down from his tree. He put the stove on its legs. Then he said:

"Them that takes cakes
    Which the Parsee boy bakes
        Makes dreadful mistakes."

And there was much more in that than you would think, because, five weeks later, there was a heat wave.

The Parsee boy took off his shirt.

But the rhinoceros took off his skin. He carried it over his shoulder as he came down to the beach to go in the water. In those days it buttoned underneath with three buttons.

The rhinoceros saw the Parsee boy. But he said nothing at all about the Parsee boy's cake even though he had eaten it all. Of course, he never had any manners, then, since, or henceforward.

He waddled straight into the water and blew bubbles through his nose, leaving his skin on the beach.

The Parsee boy looked at the skin, and he smiled one smile that ran all round his face two times. Then he danced three times round the skin and rubbed his hands.

He ran to his camp and filled his hat with cake crumbs, for the Parsee boy never ate anything but cake, and he never swept out his camp. Carrying his hatful of crumbs, he ran back to the beach where the rhinoceros had left his skin.

Then he took that skin, and he shook that skin. He scrubbed that skin, and he rubbed that skin just as full of old, dry, stale cake crumbs as ever it could possibly hold.

Still smiling, he climbed to the top of a tree and waited for the rhinoceros to come out of the water and put it on.

And the rhinoceros did. He buttoned it up with the three buttons, and it tickled like cake crumbs in bed.

Then he wanted to scratch. But that made it worse. Then he lay down on the sands and rolled and rolled and rolled, and every time he rolled, the cake crumbs tickled him worse and worse and worse.

So he ran to the tree and rubbed himself against it. He rubbed so much and so hard that he rubbed his skin into a great fold over his shoulders, and another fold underneath, where the buttons used to be. But he rubbed the buttons off. And he rubbed some more folds over his legs.

But all that rubbing didn't make one bit of difference to the cake crumbs.

195

The crumbs were inside his skin.
And they tickled! So he went home,
very angry indeed and terribly
scratchy.

And from that day to this, every
rhinoceros has great folds in his
skin and a very bad temper, all
because of the cake crumbs inside.

The Miller, His Son, and the Donkey

from

AESOP'S FABLES

 miller and his son were walking their donkey to market. They had not gone far when they passed a group of girls.

The girls stopped them and said, "Only fools walk when they could ride. Your donkey should be carrying one of you on its back."

"True enough," said the miller, nodding, so he told his son to get on the donkey's back and along they went, one walking and one riding.

197

Soon they met some old friends who looked at the son and said, "A fine son you are—fine, indeed! No son worth his salt would ride while his father goes on foot!"

"True enough," said the son, and he got off quickly and made his father get on the donkey's back.

The miller had not been riding long when they passed two boys. "That is not fair," they heard one boy say to the other.

"When one can ride but one must walk, it is always the father who gets the seat, and that is not fair!"

"True enough," said the miller. "Climb on, my son, and ride together with me. We will *both* ride."

But before long a woman stopped them. "Have you no feeling for your little donkey?" she asked. "The animal is not strong enough to carry such a heavy pair.

The two of you would be better able to carry the poor donkey than he is to carry both of you."

"True enough," said the miller and his son, wanting to do right by their donkey.

So, they got off and cut a long pole. Next they took some rope and tied the donkey's feet to the pole. Then the miller and his son lifted the pole to their shoulders so that they could carry the donkey.

And so they walked, down the road and onto the bridge, with the donkey hanging between them. Some children followed them, laughing at the silly sight.

As the miller and his son reached the middle of the bridge, the donkey kicked off his ropes. He fell from the pole into the river and was carried away by the water.

"That goes to show you," said one of the children.

**"Try to please everybody,
and you will please nobody."**

Spider and the Sticky Man

from an

AFRICAN LEGEND

pider was tricky and clever. But lazy. Very lazy! He thought it was great fun to outsmart others, and he worked hard at playing tricks.

But he was always trying to get around working in the fields with the yam farmers. Spider loved to eat yams, but the digging and planting and weeding were not as much fun as the eating.

Each year, when the planting season came to the bush lands, everyone was hard at work. Everyone, that is, except Spider.

He did not like to work. He liked to lie in the hammock he wove for himself. When all the other farmers were in their fields, clearing the weeds and planting vine cuttings, he would just stay in his hammock and sleep late.

Most days Spider was not up and around until afternoon. And then, did he get right to work? No. Then, he would have a good meal of yams and just sit in the sunshine.

His wife knew that their neighbors were working on their farms, for it was time to plant. Each day she hoped he would get to work.

Trying to get him started, she would say, "Spider, dear, don't you think it's time to get the ground ready for planting? Just tell me when you want my help with the digging."

Spider would answer, "Oh, there's lots of time yet."

But, as the days went by, he knew he would have to pretend to be doing his planting, so he would tell his wife each afternoon that he was going to work on the farm.

But he would really just keep walking until he was out of sight. Then each day Spider wove a new hammock for himself, hung it between two trees, and took a nap until sunset.

This went on all through planting time. Then came the long months of growing, and then it was time to harvest the yams.

Other farmers were bringing home their harvest, but Spider brought home nothing.

At last, his wife said, "Surely our yams are ready by now. Nearly everyone else is harvesting."

Now Spider was indeed in a fix. How could he

bring home yams when he had not done any planting? He lay awake, wondering what to do. In the middle of the night he got an idea.

Spider slipped out of the house and made his way to the biggest farm nearby. This was the chief's farm. The chief had a big field, filled with row after row of yams, not yet harvested.

As quietly as he could, Spider filled his bag with these yams. Then, after hiding the bag in a tree, he returned home.

The next morning he said to his wife, "Today I am going to start harvesting our yams."

"Good!" exclaimed his wife, little knowing what Spider was up to.

He went straight to the patch of trees where he had hidden the bag. There he sat down and wove himself a soft web-like net for his hammock, and he slept the day away.

When he came home that evening, he handed her the bag. She cooked the yams, and they tasted wonderful.

That night, and a number of the following nights, Spider went back to the chief's farm. Each time, he filled his bag with yams and hid the bag.

When morning came, he pretended to go to his farm. But he really just slept and returned to his wife in the evening.

After a time, the chief noticed that someone was taking his yams. He decided to catch the thief, so he took some large pots and went into the bush.

Soon he found the trees he was looking for. Making long cuts in the bark, he left a pot at the foot of each tree to catch the sap. The next day when he returned, he saw that his pots were full of rich brown sap. It was heavy and soft, like clay, and it was as sticky as tar.

He took the pots back to his farm. The sap was still soft enough for him to work it into the shape of a man. When it became a bit harder, he placed his man in the middle of the field where the yams were growing.

Then the chief rubbed his hands together and said to himself, "Ha! Now I shall soon know who the thief is!"

When all was dark, Spider slipped out of his house again and made his way to the chief's farm. He was just about to begin digging when he saw what he thought was a man only a few yards away.

"Oh!" he exclaimed. "Who are you?"

There was no answer.

"What do you want?" Spider asked, a little louder.

The man did not speak.

Spider took a step toward him. "What are you doing here in the middle of the night?"

But there was still no answer.

Spider was frightened and angry. Lifting his hand, he hit the man a hard blow on the face, saying, "Why don't you answer me?"

Now the man had been standing in the hot sun all day, so he was very sticky. Spider found that he could not pull his hand away from the man's face.

"Let me go at once," Spider shouted, and he hit him with the other hand.

Now Spider was really in a fix, as both hands were stuck. He began to think that there was something strange about this man.

Lifting his knees, he tried to free himself by pushing them against the man's body, only to find that they too were held fast.

Then wildly he pounded his head against the man's chest. And now he could not move at all!

"What a fool I am!" he cried. "I shall have to stay

here all night, and everyone will know I'm a thief."

Sure enough, when morning came, the chief hurried out to see who had been caught. How he laughed when he saw Spider stuck to the man—head, hands, knees, and all.

"So you were the thief!" he exclaimed. "I might have guessed it."

Poor Spider! The chief had a time of it, pulling him off the sticky man. Spider felt so bad when everyone laughed at him that he ran off to hide.

He wove another web for himself, bigger than his old hammock, and he hung it high in a corner of his house. For a long time he would see and speak to nobody. He really tried to keep out of sight.

And ever since then, the spiders that came after him have tried to keep out of sight too. They spin their webs high in corners and hide from everyone.

Arachne's Weaving

from a myth by

OVID

Long ago in the land near Mount Olympus there lived a girl named Arachne. She was a wonderful weaver. People came from far and near to see pictures take shape on her cloth.

One woman clapped as she watched Arachne's fingers fly. "How lovely!" she exclaimed. "The goddess Minerva, the mother of all weavers, must have touched Arachne's hands."

"Yes," said another. "Only with the help of a goddess could she weave so well."

But Arachne was proud. She tossed her head. "No one has ever helped me with my weaving," she said, "for no one can weave as well as I."

One day an old woman in a long black coat came to see Arachne's weaving. "This is beautiful cloth, my child," said the woman. "Only Minerva herself could do better."

"Could she?" said Arachne. "I wonder." She stepped back and looked at her work proudly. "I don't think Minerva could do better. I don't think she could do as well."

That second, the long black coat fell from the shoulders of the old woman. As she stepped forth, tall and beautiful, her hair turned from gray to gold, and there stood the great goddess Minerva.

"I will take on your challenge, Arachne," said the goddess. "And let this be a lesson to those who would challenge a goddess."

So Arachne and Minerva began to weave.

Arachne's cloth was beautiful indeed. It showed the colors of the earth, bright and clear, the green of the grass, the brown of the trees, and the reds and yellows of flowers.

But Minerva's cloth held the gold of the sun and the silver of the moon. It stretched out into a picture of Mount Olympus, so great and bright that tears came to Arachne's eyes as she looked upon it.

She knew then that she could never weave better than the goddess Minerva. Indeed, she knew that she could never weave as well. Arachne hid her face in her cloth and cried.

Then the goddess Minerva laid her hands upon the girl. "Arachne," she said. "You love to weave, so I will let you weave forever. But no longer can you make cloth. You will weave from morning until night, but you will do a different kind of weaving."

Under the hands of the goddess, Arachne grew smaller and smaller. At last she changed into a spider. Minerva made her the mother of all spiders.

And that is how it came to be that spiders work at their weaving from morning until night, and make such wonderful webs.

A Wolf and Little Daughter

by

VIRGINIA HAMILTON

ne day Little Daughter was pickin some flowers. There was a fence around the house she lived in with her papa. Papa didn't want Little Daughter to run in the forest, where there were wolves. He told Little Daughter never to go out the gate alone.

"Oh, I won't, Papa," said Little Daughter.

One mornin her papa had to go away for somethin. And Little Daughter thought she'd go huntin for flowers. She just thought it wouldn't harm anythin to peep through the gate. And that's what she did. She saw a wild yellow flower so near to the gate that she stepped outside and picked it.

Little Daughter was outside the fence now. She saw another pretty flower. She skipped over and got it, held it in her hand. It smelled sweet. She saw another and she got it, too. Put it with the others. She was makin a pretty bunch to put in her vase for the table. And so Little Daughter got farther and farther away from the cabin. She picked the flowers, and the whole time she sang a sweet song.

All at once Little Daughter heard a noise. She looked up and saw a great big wolf. The wolf said to her, in a low, gruff voice, said, "Sing that sweetest, goodest song again."

So the little child sang it, sang,

"Tray-bla, tray-bla, cum qua, kimo."

And, *pit-a-pat, pit-a-pat, pit-a-pat, pit-a-pat,* Little Daughter tiptoed toward the gate. She's goin back home. But she hears big and heavy, PIT-A-PAT, PIT-A-PAT, comin behind her. And there's the wolf. He says, "Did you move?" in a gruff voice.

Little Daughter says, "Oh, no, dear wolf, what occasion have I to move?"

"Well, sing that sweetest, goodest song again," says the wolf.

Little Daughter sang it:

"Tray-bla, tray-bla, cum qua, kimo."

And the wolf is gone again.

The child goes back some more, *pit-a-pat, pit-a-pat, pit-a-pat,* softly on tippy-toes toward the gate.

But she soon hears very loud, PIT-A-PAT, PIT-A-PAT, comin behind her. And there is the great big wolf, and he says to her, says, "I think you moved."

"Oh, no, dear wolf," Little Daughter tells him, "what occasion have I to move?"

So he says, "Sing that sweetest, goodest song again."

Little Daughter begins:

"Tray-bla, tray-bla, tray-bla, cum qua, kimo."

The wolf is gone.

But, PIT-A-PAT, PIT-A-PAT, PIT-A-PAT, comin on behind her. There's the wolf. He says to her, says, "You moved."

She says, "Oh, no, dear wolf, what occasion have I to move?"

"Sing that sweetest, goodest song again," says the big, bad wolf.

She sang:

"Tray bla-tray, tray bla-tray, tra-bla-cum qua, kimo."

The wolf is gone again.

And she, Little Daughter, *pit-a-pat, pit-a-pat, pit-a-pat*tin away home. She is so close to the gate now. And this time she hears PIT-A-PAT, PIT-A-PAT, PIT-A-PAT comin on *quick* behind her.

Little Daughter slips inside the gate. She shuts it—CRACK! PLICK!—right in that big, bad wolf's face.

She sweetest, goodest safe!

215

Sergei Prokofiev was a Russian composer and pianist. In 1936 he wrote the words and music for a fairy tale called "Peter and the Wolf."

Every character in the story is represented by a different instrument in the orchestra.

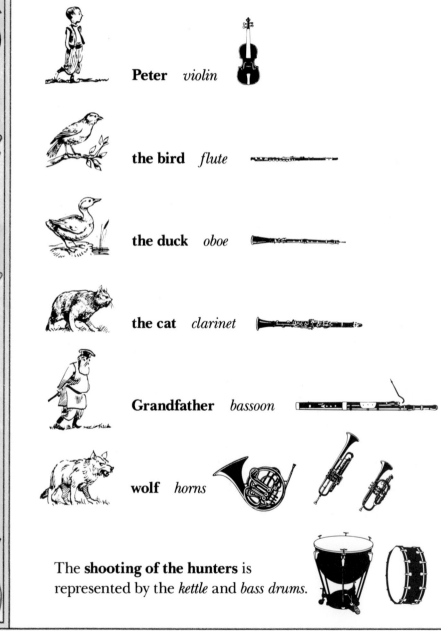

Peter   *violin*

the bird   *flute*

the duck   *oboe*

the cat   *clarinet*

Grandfather   *bassoon*

wolf   *horns*

The **shooting of the hunters** is represented by the *kettle* and *bass drums*.

Peter and the Wolf

by

SERGEI PROKOFIEV

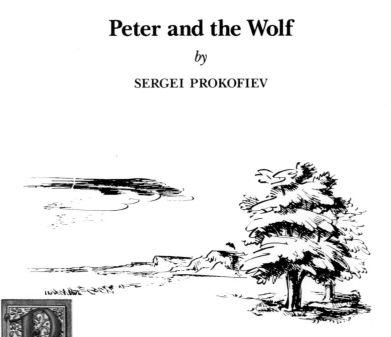

eter and his grandfather lived beside a
beautiful sunny meadow in a great forest. In this
meadow was a pond where Peter sometimes fed
the ducks.

But his grandfather did not like him to go to
that pond. His grandfather was afraid to let Peter
go outside their fence.

"Peter," Grandfather would say, "stay here in our
garden. Don't go wandering around the meadow.
What if a wolf should come out of the forest?"

Now, Peter did not think that a wolf was anything
to be afraid of, and the pond was just a little way
outside the fence. So off he went to feed the ducks.

As he reached the pond, Peter saw his friend the bird singing at the top of a big tree.

Soon after, a duck came waddling through the meadow to swim in the pond.

As soon as the little bird saw the duck, he began to argue with her.

"What kind of bird are you if you can't fly?" said the bird, and he flew in a circle over the duck's head.

"Well, what kind of bird are you if you can't swim in the pond?" said the duck, and she swam in a circle in the water.

The little bird landed on the bank of the pond.

He hopped along as he argued with the duck.

Then, out of the corner of his eye, Peter saw something move. It was the cat, creeping through the grass, getting closer and closer and closer to the bird.

The cat said to herself, "Ah, I will have that bird for my dinner!" She crept toward him on her soft paws.

"Look out!" cried Peter.

The cat sprang just as Peter shouted, but the bird was quick. That second, he flew up into the tree, and he chirped for joy at being out of the reach of the cat.

Just then Peter's grandfather called to him from the gate, "How many times have I told you not to go past our fence and into the meadow?"

Grandfather went on, "It isn't safe. I once saw a wolf in this meadow, so get back to the garden, Peter, right now."

Slowly Peter walked back to the gate, kicking a stone in front of him. Then he just stood there, watching the animals, while his grandfather walked toward the house.

And what should Peter see that very minute but a wolf coming out of the forest! A big, hungry-looking wolf!

Peter watched the wolf cross the meadow, running quietly through the tall grass, coming closer. No sooner had Peter's grandfather gone inside and shut the door than the wolf was at the pond.

The cat saw him coming. In a flash she ran up the tree and sprang onto the first branch.

The bird flew out to the end of that branch, chirping at the duck. "Watch out!" he called.

The duck was so frightened that she stopped swimming and just quacked. Then she lost her head altogether, and flapped out of the pond and up onto the bank.

No matter how hard the duck tried to run, she could not get away from the wolf. With one quick leap, he was upon her, and he swallowed her whole.

But the wolf was still hungry. As he looked about for more to eat, the cat and the bird caught his eye. He leaped at them, but their branch was too high for him.

The cat stayed as still as stone, staring down at the wolf. The bird flew to another branch, not too close to the cat.

Peter stayed at the gate, watching all that was going on. Quickly he decided what to do. First he got a rope. Then he climbed up onto his fence. From there, he could grab hold of a branch of the tree that held the cat and the bird. He climbed onto that branch, and from there higher into the tree.

Peter tied a knot in one end of the rope to make a lasso. Then he said to the bird, "Fly down, and circle close to the wolf's head, but be careful. Don't let him get you with those sharp teeth of his. I mean to catch him while he is trying to catch you."

Bravely, the bird flew down. The wolf snapped at him from this side and that. He flew close again and again, but stayed just out of reach. Once he almost touched the wolf's ear with his wing.

And how that did worry the wolf! Hungry and angry, he threw himself around, snapping at the bird. Oh, how he wanted to catch him and swallow him!

Meanwhile, Peter let down his lasso. He worked it closer and closer to the wolf's tail. Then, with one quick move, he slid the knot tight, and the wolf found himself pulled off his back feet.

He howled wildly, trying to get loose. Peter's grandfather came running out of the house, and out from the forest came two hunters who had been trailing the wolf.

Everyone was shouting, but Peter loudest of all.

"We caught the wolf," he cried. "The bird and I! We did it! Let's take him to the zoo."

Then it was like a parade. Peter smiled a proud smile as he walked at the head of the line. Next came the hunters, cheering and laughing, with the wolf who was still howling.

After them followed Peter's grandfather. Again and again he shook his head.

"But what if the lasso had not worked," asked Grandfather, "and what if Peter had fallen out of the tree?" But nobody answered him.

Then came the cat with its tail in the air, and bringing up the end of the parade was the bird, chirping happily, "Aren't we smart! See who we caught!"

And if you listened very carefully, you could hear one other sound. It was the quacking of the duck in the wolf's stomach. He had swallowed her whole, so she was still alive and making herself heard in this happy parade.

Do-Re-Mi

from

THE SOUND OF MUSIC

by

OSCAR HAMMERSTEIN *and* RICHARD RODGERS

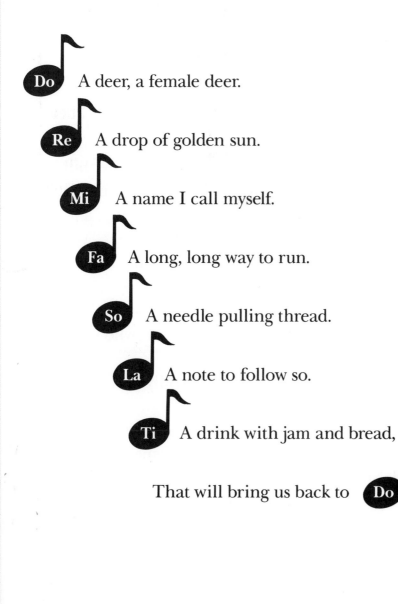

Do A deer, a female deer.

Re A drop of golden sun.

Mi A name I call myself.

Fa A long, long way to run.

So A needle pulling thread.

La A note to follow so.

Ti A drink with jam and bread,

That will bring us back to **Do**

225

His First Bronc

from

YOUNG COWBOY

by

WILL JAMES

ne day Billy's father, Lem, told him he could have a certain horse if he could break him in. It was a little black horse, pretty as a picture. Billy was a born cowboy. He went wild at the sight of the horse, and ran into the corral to get as close a look at him as he could.

"By golly," he said, "I've always wanted to break in a horse. That'll be lots of fun."

"Maybe," said his father, "but this one bucks a lot. He's thrown two or three ranch hands who tried to break him in."

The next morning Lem found Billy in the corral with the new horse.

"Well, son, I see you're busy right early," said Lem.

"You bet, Dad," said Billy. "He's some horse!"

"He sure is," agreed Lem. "He's a real bucking bronco, and your first bronc, too."

An hour or so later Billy had his saddle on
the black horse, strapped on to stay. By this time
a few of the cowboys had gathered around
to watch.

Some of the men had told Billy they'd help him,
but that young cowboy wanted to do it all himself.
It was his bronc.

Billy gathered his rope, grabbed the saddle horn
with his right hand, and moved himself slow and
easy. He was onto the horse, and he was ready for
whatever happened.

The pony just looked back at the boy sitting on him, tossed his head, and trotted off.

A laugh went up from all around. Billy turned a surprised face toward his father and yelled, "Hey, Dad, he won't buck."

Another laugh was heard, and when it quieted down, Lem spoke up. "Never mind, son," he said, trying to keep a straight face. "He might buck yet."

The words were no more than out of his mouth when the little black horse lit into bucking. Billy slipped to the side on the first jump, for he'd been paying more mind to what his dad was saying than to what he was sitting on.

The little pony crow-hopped around the corral and bucked just enough to keep Billy from getting straight in the saddle again. But Billy hung on, and pretty soon he got his seat pretty well under him.

Then he tried to do a little showing-off. He grabbed his hat and started waving it. The horse bucked. Up and up went Billy, a little higher each time the horse jumped.

And on the highest buck, when Billy came down, the horse wasn't there. Billy was by his lonesome

on the ground. The horse was on the other side
of the corral.

"Where is he?" said Billy, trying to get some
of the earth out of his eyes.

"Right here, son," said his father who had caught
the horse and brought him up. "Are you ready for
more, cowboy?"

Billy nodded.

His father held the horse while Billy climbed
on again.

"Let him go, Dad."

The pony lit into bucking as soon as he was loose
this time. He seemed to mean to throw Billy from
the start.

Billy was doing mighty fine at first, but the
bronco didn't let up. Then Billy kept getting farther
and farther away from the saddle. Finally he slid
along the pony's shoulder and down to the ground
once again.

He was up before his dad could get to him.
He began walking toward his horse right away.

"Maybe that's enough for today, son," Lem said
as he brushed off Billy's shirt. "Maybe tomorrow
you can ride him easy."

But Billy turned and saw the horse challenging him, it seemed. "One more try," he said as he crossed the corral.

"Well," said Lem, "one more try might do it. You go after him this time, Billy. You make this pony think you're the wolf of the world."

Billy climbed on. "Y-e-e-p!" he yelled as the bronc started bucking. "I'm a wolf!"

Billy was a wolf! He was going to show this horse who was boss. He had turned into the challenger, and he had a feeling that the horse could tell.

Again and again daylight showed between Billy and the saddle, but somehow he was sticking on and staying right side up.

The horse, surprised at the change, finally let up on his bucking. He seemed to sense that something was different, and he was getting scared. That little pony found a sudden hankering to stop bucking and start running.

After that it was easy for Billy. He rode him around the corral a few times. Then, all smiles and proud as could be, he climbed off.

Billy had broken in his first bronc.

Buckin' Bronco

by

SHEL SILVERSTEIN

Can you ride the buckin' bronco?
Can you stay in that ol' saddle
Till your teeth begin to rattle?
Can you whoop and bounce
And stick upon his back?

Can you ride the buckin' bronco
While he's snortin' smoke and kickin'
And your stomach starts to sicken
And you feel as though
Your spine's about to crack?

I can ride the buckin' bronco,
I'll just sit up here and whistle
Till his strength begins to fizzle
And he knows that I'm
His master finally.

Yes I'll tame the buckin' bronco,
You can see me settin' easy.
Here's the buckin' bronco,
                    Here is me. →

Every Time I Climb a Tree

by

DAVID McCORD

Every time I climb a tree
Every time I climb a tree
Every time I climb a tree
I scrape a leg
Or skin a knee
And every time I climb a tree
I find some ants
Or dodge a bee
And get the ants
All over me.

And every time I climb a tree
Where have you been?
They say to me.
But don't they know that I am free
Every time I climb a tree?
I like it best
To spot a nest
That has an egg
Or maybe three.

And then I skin
The other leg,
But every time I climb a tree
I see a lot of things to see
Swallows, rooftops, and TV
And all the fields and
    farms there be.

Every time I climb a tree
Though climbing may be
    good for ants
It isn't awfully good for pants
But still it's pretty good for me
Every time I climb a tree.

235

Gulliver's Travels in Lilliput

from

GULLIVER'S TRAVELS

by

JONATHAN SWIFT

or many years I sailed the seas, working as a ship's doctor. I could help sailors who were sick. But I was of little help in a storm, and it was a wild storm that drove my ship off course and led to my strange adventures in the Land of Lilliput.

When the storm was at its wildest, my ship crashed against a huge rock, and water rushed in through the hole.

"Dr. Gulliver!" a sailor called to me. "We're sinking!"

The sailors let down a small boat over the side of the ship. "Get in!" they shouted. I did as they said, but soon our little boat was upset by the waves.

What became of those good sailors, I cannot tell, but I suppose they were all lost. For my own part, I was pushed forward by the wind and waves. I often let my legs drop, and could feel no bottom. But when I was almost gone, and able to swim no longer, I found my feet touching the bottom.

I walked nearly a mile before I reached land. I then walked half a mile, but saw no houses or people.

237

I was very tired and felt a great need for sleep, so I lay down on the grass. There, I slept sounder than I ever remember having done in my life.

When I woke up, I was lying on my back. It was daylight. I tried to move, but could not. My arms and legs were tied on each side to the ground, and my long hair was tied down in the same way.

I could only look up. The sun was hot, and the light hurt my eyes. I heard a noise about me, but from where I lay, I could see nothing except the sky.

Then I felt something moving up my left leg. I tried to lift my head, but my hair was tied down too tightly. I tried to move my leg. Whatever was moving upon me stopped. It seemed to be waiting to see what I would do.

I lay still. Then it moved again. It walked over my body and came almost up to my chest. I turned my eyes down as much as I could. Looking down over my chin, I could just catch sight of what was walking over me, and I could not believe my eyes!

It was a tiny man, not as tall as my hand. He was holding a bow and arrow. The arrow was about as big as a pin, and he was pointing it at me.

I felt more of these tiny men walking upon me.

I was so surprised, and roared so loudly, that they all ran back, frightened.

They soon returned, and one of them came up to my face. He lifted his hands and cried, "Heka degul."

The others said the same words, but at that time I knew not what they meant.

I lay all this while worried about being tied down. At last I broke the strings that held my left arm to the ground. Then, with a strong pull, I loosened the strings that tied down my hair on the right side. This allowed me to turn my head a bit.

I reached for the tiny men nearest to me, but they ran off, shouting.

Then I heard a man cry loudly, "Tolo fonac."

In a second, about a hundred arrows hit my left hand. They felt like the tips of so many pins sticking me, and they burned like fire.

Then again, I heard, "Tolo fonac."

The next rain of arrows fell on my face, which I quickly covered with my hand. At that point I thought it was wisest to lie still and wait until dark to try to free myself.

But as soon as the people saw that I was quiet, they stopped shooting arrows. By the noise I heard,

I knew that many of them had set to work about four yards from my right ear. I turned my head that way, as far as the strings holding my hair would allow.

They had built a stage, about a foot and a half from the ground. One of them climbed a ladder to the stage and started to speak to me. I could not understand his words, but I could tell from his voice that he was sometimes warning, sometimes promising, sometimes asking. When he finished, he seemed to be waiting for me to reply.

I answered in a few words, but I knew he could not understand me. So, being terribly hungry, I tried putting my fingers to my mouth, over and over again, to try to show him that I needed food.

He understood me. He had some ladders placed against my side. Lines of tiny men climbed up and walked toward my mouth, carrying baskets of food. As soon as I emptied one basket, I was given another.

I later found out that wagons of meat and bread had been sent by the king when he heard about me.

For meat, there were tiny shoulders and legs, shaped like those of sheep and cows. They were very well cooked, but smaller than the wing of a bird. I ate them two or three at a bite, bones and all.

Their loaves of bread were not as big as the tip of my finger. I put them into my mouth, three at a time.

The people could not believe how much I ate!

I made a sign that I wanted a drink.

They let down ropes and pulled up some barrels. Each one was about half as big as a cup.

I drank the first barrel at once, and made signs for more. They brought me more barrels, which I drank in the same manner. They kept on pulling up barrels until I had all I wanted to drink.

After some time, when they saw that I asked for no more food, there came before me a person sent by the king. This person spoke for about ten minutes, often pointing forward. He seemed to be trying to tell me where I was to go.

In answer, I made a sign with my hand that was loose. I put it to my other hand. Then I touched my head and body, to mean that I wanted to be untied.

He shook his head. Then he showed me by signs that I could not be let loose because his people were afraid of me, so I must be carried in a huge wagon that they were building for me. He made other signs to let me understand that I should have food and drink enough, and that they would not hurt me.

I again thought of trying to break free. But I still felt the burning of their arrows upon my face and hands, and there were hundreds of tiny bowmen all around me, so I made signs to let them know that they might do with me what they pleased.

Soon after, they rubbed my face and hands with something that had a sweet smell. It took away all the burning of their arrows.

Then sleep came upon me. I knew nothing of what was happening to me for the next ten hours.

It seems that as soon as I was found in Lilliput, the king ordered that I should be tied down. But he also made plans to have food and drink brought to me and a wagon built to carry me to his city.

The people of Lilliput are great builders—of roads, ships, castles. They have built machines on wheels for carrying heavy loads. So they quickly built a wagon seven feet long and four feet wide for me.

The hardest part, they knew, would be to raise me off the ground and place me in it. So nine hundred men worked together with ropes and pulleys. They tied their strongest ropes around my neck, arms, legs, and body, and in three hours they had picked me up and swung me over into the wagon.

I was told all of this later, when I learned the language spoken in Lilliput. I knew nothing of it while it was happening, for I was in a deep sleep. The people of Lilliput had made sure I would sleep through their work. They mixed their strongest sleeping medicines with the water they gave me.

When I woke up and looked about me, I found that I was in an old temple. It was the biggest building in Lilliput, and it was to be my home. Across the road from this temple was a castle about five feet high. The king and queen and their followers had climbed to the roof of this castle to get a good look at me.

The king's men put chains around my left leg. Each chain was six feet long, but only about as heavy as the chains ladies wear around their necks in my country. They put a hundred of these chains on my leg, to keep me from breaking loose.

Then they cut all my ropes. Once more I could sit up. How good it felt to stretch! But what a noise the people made when they saw me lift my arms straight up! And how they ran when I stood up and took the few steps my chains would let me take!

Standing up, I could see much of their city and countryside. Their tallest trees were about as tall as I was. Their houses looked like doll houses.

The sound of horns let me know the king was ready to speak with me. He spoke clearly, and I replied. But we could not understand each other.

Three men came forward and tried to talk with me. These, I guessed, were teachers who knew other languages. They said many strange-sounding words, and I spoke back in all the languages I knew. But we were able to understand each other only through signs.

At last, they made me understand that they would help me learn their language, and they came back each day to teach me. I did well and could soon speak with them and understand all that was said to me.

•   •   •   •

That was the start of Gulliver's adventures in the land of Lilliput. *Gulliver's Travels* was first printed in 1726, and readers still like it today.

Gulliver

by

BILL HOEST

"Let's not be hasty, sire . . . We can use him for our
university basketball team!"

The Swing

by

ROBERT LOUIS STEVENSON

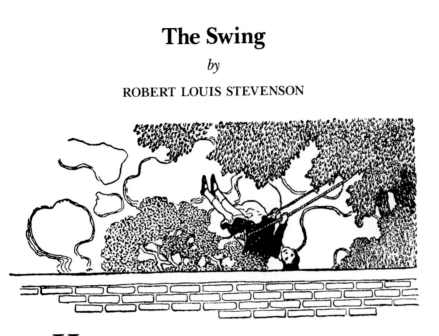

How do you like to go up in a swing,
Up in the air so blue?
Oh, I do think it's the pleasantest thing
Ever a child can do!

Up in the air and over the wall,
Till I can see so wide,
Rivers and trees and cattle and all
Over the countryside.

Till I look down on the garden green,
Down on the roof so brown—
Up in the air I go flying again,
Up in the air and down!

Afternoon on a Hill

by

EDNA ST. VINCENT MILLAY

I will be the gladdest thing
    Under the sun!
I will touch a hundred flowers
    And not pick one.

I will look at cliffs and clouds
    With quiet eyes,
Watch the wind bow down the grass,
    And the grass rise.

And when the lights begin to show
    Up from the town,
I will mark which must be mine,
    And then start down!

A·C·K·N·O·W·L·E·D·G·M·E·N·T·S

Acknowledgment is gratefully made to the following individuals and publishers for permission to reprint these selections.

"Bambi's Questions." From *Bambi* by Felix Salten. © 1928, 1956 by Simon & Schuster, Inc. Reprinted by permission of Simon & Schuster, Inc.

"Good Advice." Every effort has been made to locate the copyright holder of this poem.

"Adventures of Isabel." Excerpt of "Adventures of Isabel" from *Custard and Company* by Ogden Nash. © 1936 by Ogden Nash. Reprinted by permission of Little, Brown and Company.

"Hope." From *Selected Poems of Langston Hughes.* © 1942 by Alfred A. Knopf, Inc. and renewed 1970 by Arna Bontemps and George Houston Bass. Reprinted by permission of Alfred A. Knopf, Inc.

"The Life of a Man Is a Circle." From *Black Elk Speaks* by John G. Neihardt, © John G. Neihardt, published by the University of Nebraska Press.

"Dust of Snow." From *The Poetry of Robert Frost,* edited by Edward Connery Lathem. © 1923, 1969 by Holt, Rinehart and Winston, Inc. © 1936, 1951 by Robert Frost. © 1964 by Lesley Frost Ballantine. Reprinted by permission of Henry Holt and Company, Inc.

"The Pale Pink Dog." From *Henry Huggins* by Beverly Cleary. © 1950 by Beverly Cleary. Reprinted by permission of Morrow Junior Books, a division of William Morrow & Company.

"The Young Puppy." © A. A. Milne. Reprinted by permission of Curtis Brown, London.

"Pecos Bill and His Pony." Excerpt from "Pecos Bill and His Bouncing Bride" from *Yankee Doodle's Cousins* by Anne Malcolmson. © 1941 by Anne Burnett Malcolmson. © renewed 1969 by Anne Malcolmson von Storch. Reprinted by permission of Houghton Mifflin Company.

I·L·L·U·S·T·R·A·T·I·O·N C·R·E·D·I·T·S

PAGE	ILLUSTRATOR
11, 17	Courtesy of Christie's East, New York. © Walt Disney Studios.
12–16	Thomas Ewing Malloy. © 1991 by Jamestown Publishers, Inc. All rights reserved.
18, 27	Fritz Eichenberg. Reprinted by permission of Fritz Eichenberg © 1945. Courtesy of the Kerlan Collection, Walter Library, University of Minnesota, Minneapolis.
19, 21, 24–25	Fritz Eichenberg. Reprinted by permission of Grosset & Dunlap, Inc. from *Black Beauty, the Autobiography of a Horse* by Anna Sewell. © 1945, © renewed 1973 by Grosset & Dunlap, Inc.
29	Milo Winter. From *The Aesop for Children*, illustrated by Milo Winter. © 1919, 1947 Checkerboard Press, a division of Macmillan, Inc. All rights reserved.
30	Tom Feelings. © by Tom Feelings.
32–33, 35–36, 39, 42, 44	Pamela R. Levy. © 1991 by Jamestown Publishers, Inc. All rights reserved.
41	Arthur Rackham.

108–109	J. W. Vawter.
111–114	Shonto Begay. © 1991 by Jamestown Publishers, Inc. All rights reserved.
117	N. C. Wyeth. Courtesy of the Free Library of Philadelphia.
121, 125, 129	Timothy C. Jones. © 1991 by Jamestown Publishers, Inc. All rights reserved.
131	Bill Watterson.
132	N. C. Wyeth. Oil on canvas, 1917. Collection of The New York Public Library, Central Children's Room, Donnell Library Center. Photograph courtesy of the Brandywine River Museum.
133–145	Pamela R. Levy. © 1991 by Jamestown Publishers, Inc. All rights reserved.
147	Paul Goble. © 1991 by Paul Goble.
148	Katharine Sturges.
151, 154	Bob Eggleton. © 1991 by Jamestown Publishers, Inc. All rights reserved.
156	Milo Winter. From *The Aesop for Children,* illustrated by Milo Winter. © 1919, 1947 Checkerboard Press, a division of Macmillan, Inc. All rights reserved.
158–159	Lilian Obligado. © 1991 by Jamestown Publishers, Inc. All rights reserved.
161–187	W. W. Denslow.
190–191	Thomas Ewing Malloy. © 1991 by Jamestown Publishers, Inc. All rights reserved.